Praise for *SuperCycles*

"*SuperCycles* provides a rich antidote to orthodox thinking about contemporary global imbalances and today's financial crisis, and as such is a must-read for policymakers and investors. Arun Motianey challenges neoclassical orthodoxy in macroeconomics by providing a historical analysis of relative price shocks, which typically have their root in commodities.

"This insightful and engaging book demonstrates how disinflation can have entrenched malignant effects and can ultimately be combated only with pro-inflation policies. By revealing how booms build on busts (the Roaring '20s, Japan in the '80s, tech in the '90s, and our recent credit boom), he provides us with a new way to look at and understand where we find ourselves today. Not all readers will agree with the author's savage criticism of the finance-driven modern economy, but few will read the book without having at least some of their preconceived notions challenged."

—Dr. Kevin Hebner, Global Investment Strategist,
Third Wave Global Investors

"Arun Motianey is one of the smartest people I know. He has the uncanny ability to see the broad movements. This book is important for those who do not want to get lulled into the conventional thinking."

—David Martin, Chief Risk Officer, Alliance Bernstein

"In this book Arun Motianey shines a searchlight on some of the more ludicrous propositions of modern equilibrium economics. He goes on to describe how investment bankers invented financial products designed to make the real world look like the economists' model. Both the economists and the bankers got it wrong—and the world is experiencing the disastrous consequences.

"The author proves a new way for thinking about global value creation—and destruction. His ability to move between economic theory and investment practice gives his analyses authority, while the impressive historical and geographical range of the book forces the reader repeatedly to re-examine conventional interpretations of the financial crisis."

—Dr. Terry O'Shaughnessy, Fellow in Economics,
St Anne's College, Oxford University

"Arun Motianey's *SuperCycles* provides an innovative and provocative approach to understanding the forces that are buffeting the world economy today. This lively volume not only examines the big picture, but also provides practical advice for investors who are trying to prosper in the complex and challenging economic environment that we are facing."

—Harvey S. Rosen, John L. Weinberg Professor of Economics and
Business Policy, Princeton University

"Motianey's thoughtful and innovative concept of rolling deflations is a provocative way of looking at the global economy. This is a thought-provoking book that will make you stop and think."

—Peter Scaturro, Private Bank Executive

"Combining wit, erudition, and practical investment insight, Arun Motianey revs up the engines to take us on a supercharged ride through the whirlwind of the great global financial crisis. This remarkable and highly readable volume is the pitch-perfect blend of the best economic thinking informed by the lessons from the past and the investment savvy of a veteran investment advisor riding high at the top of his game.

"Students and teachers of economics and finance will benefit enormously from this text. So, too, will legions of perplexed investors anxiously awaiting the next twists and turns of the SuperCycle. Neither they nor the rest of us can know what surprises lie in wait for our battered portfolios as this journey unfolds, but thanks to Motianey, we have a crystal clear idea of where we are at the start."

—Thomas J. Trebat, Executive Director, Institute of
Latin American Studies & Center for Brazilian Studies,
Columbia University

SuperCycles

SuperCycles

THE NEW ECONOMIC FORCE
TRANSFORMING GLOBAL MARKETS
AND INVESTMENT STRATEGY

ARUN MOTIANEY

New York   Chicago   San Francisco   Lisbon
London   Madrid   Mexico City   Milan   New Delhi
San Juan   Seoul   Singapore   Sydney   Toronto

The McGraw·Hill Companies

Copyright © 2010 by Arun Motianey. All rights reserved. Printed in
the United States of America. Except as permitted under the United
States Copyright Act of 1976, no part of this publication may be
reproduced or distributed in any form or by any means, or stored in
a database or retrieval system, without the prior written permission
of the publisher.

1 2 3 4 5 6 7 8 9 0   DOC/DOC   1 8 7 6 5 4 3 2 1 0

ISBN 978-0-07-163737-4
MHID 0-07-163737-0

This publication is designed to provide accurate and authoritative information in regard to the subject matter covered. It is sold
with the understanding that neither the author nor the publisher is
engaged in rendering legal, accounting, futures/securities trading, or
other professional service. If legal advice or other expert assistance is
required, the services of a competent professional person should be
sought.
—*From a Declaration of Principles jointly adopted by a Committee*
of the American Bar Association and a Committee of Publishers

McGraw-Hill books are available at special quantity discounts
to use as premiums and sales promotions, or for use in corporate
training programs. To contact a representative, please e-mail us at
bulksales@mcgraw-hill.com.

This book is printed on acid-free paper.

CONTENTS

● CONTENTS ●

INTRODUCTION

Like the character Zelig in Woody Allen's eponymous film, I somehow seem to have found a seat at some of the great economic and financial crises of the last 30 years. Thankfully, it was not a ringside seat; distance allowed me to see their broad movements without losing myself in the details.

Throughout this time I was based in New York, working at Citi—initially Citicorp, then Citigroup, then just plain Citi. I owe a great debt of gratitude to my former employer, once a mighty financial empire conquering every market it encountered, but now, if some commentators are to be believed, just a sad and broken firm desperately in need of euthanasia. If I hadn't had the jobs I had in that vast international organization, I would not have had the chance to observe and sometimes participate in these events. It gave me matchless access to people and resources in every crisis-afflicted region over a 20-year period.

But even then I felt a nagging doubt toward my former colleagues—many of whom are no longer at Citi but are now in a joint venture with Morgan Stanley. In both the institutional and the wealth management businesses on Wall Street, and among their retained consultants, many of whom were former Federal Reserve officials, I encountered the worst kind of conformist thinking, recycled endlessly, sometimes ignorantly and sometimes cynically, to rationalize the industry's own feral behavior in herding investor capital into and out of these markets. Yet this is a book about economic stability, not economic justice (and unlike classically liberal economists, I believe that those two ideas should be built on entirely different philosophical foundations) so I shall restrain my expressions of moral outrage beyond this point.

SUPERCYCLES PAST AND PRESENT

Capital is a key player in this drama. SuperCycle tells Capital where to move; Capital tells SuperCycle how high to go and how far to fall. There would be no story to tell if either were missing. This is why the last 125 years has been the age of SuperCycles, *except* for that brief period between World War II and the 1971–1973 fall of the Bretton Woods system, when cross-border capital flows were small and changes in relative prices—that is, prices of commodities in terms of secondary goods and vice versa—were minor. In those years the SuperCycle was simply off the stage. The reader would do well to remember this since the features of this phenomenon that I have called the SuperCycle are understood as much by the conditions that enable them as those that suppress them.

Yet no less than a reawakened Valkyrie, the SuperCycle is lured out of its Valhalla, and something restores its potency and drives it ineluctably forward. In Wagner's *Götterdämmerung* it is Brunnhilde who, revived by her lover-to-be Siegfried, then embarks on a long journey to return the ring to the Rhinemaidens and cleanse the world of its curse. Similarly, the arrival of a new monetary standard—whether the expanded Gold Standard in 1879 or the Enlightened Fiat Standard in 1979—brings hope of price stability after a long spell of purchasing power debasement.

It sets in motion *a series of dramatic price movements* that begins with commodities, moves through manufacturing, and ends up as a crushing deadweight on the balance sheet of households in the goods-using (rather than goods-producing) economies. This is the essence of the SuperCycle—a generation-long price swing that drives the world economy from high inflation to deflation and back to inflation again with potent side effects that we recognize too often after the fact as asset bubbles. The curse of the Ring in Wagner's musical dramas is analogous to the curse of inflation in the story of the SuperCycle, neither of which can be flushed out without leaving destruction and ruin in its wake.

While most of us think instinctively in terms of specific economies in a stereotyped way—the United States as the world's largest consumer, China as a source of goods and recycled savings, the Middle East economies as the world's largest exporter of energy, and so on—the reader will be asked from time to time to temporarily suspend these conventional categories and think only in terms of a global *pipeline* or *supply chain of production*. This is easy to understand intuitively. All goods begin as commodities that are then processed through various intermediate stages of production, drawing in labor along the way, until their final stage, at which point they are consumed. (Even services can be thought of as a bundle of goods and labor— think of the X-ray machines and the radiologist who diagnoses your medical condition or the pipes and tools that the plumber uses to unclog your drains.) Most goods these days are made up of commodities that come from one region of the world, get manufactured in a different part of the world, and are mostly consumed in some other place altogether.

The SuperCycle, then, is a process of disinflation that winds its way through this global pipeline—from commodities to finished goods and services, like a pig devoured by a python—leaving convulsive booms and busts in its wake, first in commodities, then manufactured goods, and then services and consumption. *Winds its way* are the operative words: the process of disinflation is not everywhere at the same time but occurs in sequence. Eventually, however, this disinflation soon threatens to turn into deflation, and in the absence of determined stabilizing action by the authorities, the result is entrenched and irreversible deflation.

The deflation threat this book describes is far more counterintuitive than our conventional ideas would lead us to believe. Some of the most renowned economists of earlier and contemporary eras—Irving Fisher, John Maynard Keynes, Hyman Minsky, and, most recently, Ben Bernanke—have warned us of the menace of deflation in highly indebted economies. For some of them, deflation renders monetary policy impotent such that unconventional tools are necessary to rescue our economies. The extreme and unprecedented measures the Fed was forced to take in 2008 and 2009 are good recent illustrations of this thinking. But I go further in this book. I warn that the perils are so great that in fact some of the tools we use—the zero-interest-rate monetary policy in particular—don't actually save us from deflation but enmesh us in it even more deeply.

Now it is time for us to bring countries and regions back into our fleshed-out model. In this framework of a global production pipeline and the sequence of booms and busts traveling down this pipeline, we can view the lost decade of Latin America in the 1980s, the crises of the Japanese and Asian economies in the 1990s, and the near collapse of the United States, United Kingdom, and indeed the international financial system in the late first decade of the 2000s, not as separate, independent events but as *successive* points on the same extended pattern that is the SuperCycle. The (commodities-dominated) bust in Latin America necessarily fed the (manufacturing) boom in Asia just as the bust in that region fed the upward spiral in the giant services-dominated and goods-consuming economies of the developed world, most especially the U.S. and U.K. economies. And their bust is where we find ourselves today.

There have been two major SuperCycles in history. The first SuperCycle—the Classical one, which stretched for more than half a century from the widespread adoption of the Gold Standard in the 1870s to the Great Depression—ended abruptly in the early 1930s in the mass liquidation of goods-producing capacity in the gold standard economies, that is, the United States, Germany, the Scandinavian countries, and a handful of Latin American economies. The modern global economy has already had its own (arguably milder) versions of the Great Depression in the off-and-on catatonic state of the Japanese economy over the last 20 years, the fast-motion collapse in East Asia, and the slow bleed of the manufacturing sectors of the U.S. economy. In each case we forestalled the most severe effects of the 1930s—in which the economy folded in on itself—because policymakers had learned from the mistakes of the past.

The second SuperCycle—the Modern SuperCycle—which we are currently experiencing, dates to the formation of the Volcker Fed in 1979. It has proceeded much further than its predecessor, while moving much quicker. Since so many of the policy prescriptions and investment recommendations I offer in this book will stand or fall on the accuracy of this one proposition, let me forcefully repeat that last point for the sake of the reader: today the global economy is at a different, indeed later, stage of the SuperCycle than it was at the time of the Great Depression, and as such, we need new ways to meet the challenges we will confront.

But first we also need to turn one piece of conventional wisdom on its ear; namely, that our system of floating exchange rates is superior to fixed rates because it absorbs these kinds of shocks better. I shall argue that this is utterly false, and the IMF has unwittingly and in its customary shortsighted way contributed over the years to aggravating the effects of the SuperCycle.

If we lived under a pure Gold Standard regime, we would experience something like the shock from falling input prices that I have just laid out, and the world economy would experience the succession of expansions and crises I have described. Yet I am convinced that the *propagation* mechanism of the SuperCycle—the shifts in the terms of trade and the ups and downs in economic activity that have resulted from it—has been made more extreme because most economies have flexible currencies. What I am saying here is that the amplitude in output swings tends to be much greater in the floating exchange rate system. The crises tend to be deeper but the recoveries tend to be sharper. From the perspective of the individual country this is probably a good thing; from the standpoint of the SuperCycle it is unquestionably bad.

This will seem counterintuitive to most readers. Don't Gold Standard countries have to adjust to the harsh price-specie-flow arrangement whereby capital outflows reduce the money supply and hence force the sector (and the economy in question) to deflate? Didn't the in-built flaws of the Gold Standard produce the Great Depression? The answer is no to both questions; it was a breakdown in the Gold "Exchange" Standard (where payment imbalances were to be remedied by borrowing from a pool of funds created by the leading economies of the world in the mid-1920s and so obviating the need for gold to flow across borders and force adjustments of money supply) that led to the Depression. It was a failure of policy coordination—compounded by other policy mishaps in the U.S. economy in particular—and not a failure of the underlying arrangement that produced an appalling outcome.

A better way to illustrate the broader point of fixed versus floating currencies is to simply compare Malaysia and Thailand between 1997 and 2001—or Argentina and Mexico between 1995 and 2001. Unit export prices in each case fell much more sharply in the economy that had devalued its currency

(Thailand, Mexico) than in the economy that held the nominal value of its currency (Malaysia, Argentina). These falls translated into lower input costs to the foreign buyer, widening his margins more than would have been possible if the supplier was simply deflating in a fixed exchange rate regime. The problem was being handed on to the next sector in the supply chain; the terms-of-trade shock was getting magnified. Once we stop seeing crises as individual events but rather as part of the fabric that is the SuperCycle, it occurs to us that problems at each stage were simply cumulating.

The International Monetary Fund, led in each case by the Rubin-Summers-Fisher troika, acted to enforce a program of devaluations and tight monetary policy. The idea was to engineer a large real depreciation of the exchange rate in each of the crisis economies, all in the name of restoring competitiveness, and foster a quick adjustment of these countries' imbalances. The boom that would follow in the U.S. economy and elsewhere, starting from 10 years ago, was a direct consequence of these exchange rate policies and of the flawed advice given to these countries by the IMF and its supporters in the U.S. Treasury. The Modern SuperCycle had been given a powerful tailwind and so came roaring into the U.S. economy.

THE RISK OF ERRONEOUS RESPONSE

I pose the same question now that I'll also ask at various places in the book: today's policymakers seem very determined that we not misapply the solution, but are we sure we are not misdiagnosing the problem? We should ask ourselves whether *this* crisis at *this* stage requires *these* particular stabilizing responses. The heart of the book is the middle sections, II, III, and IV, and they bring the reader to the point where asking this question becomes unavoidable.

Let me not equivocate about where I stand on this. I am convinced that our policymakers simply do not understand the crisis they confront, and much of Section IV explains why. But here is a brief overview. The Great Depression taught us a few important lessons but none more important than this: the government is the shock absorber of last resort, both to catch falling demand and to be the guarantor of the financial system. This verity will be sorely tested during the current crisis, and I believe it will be found to come up short.

Transferring debt from the household sector to the government or from the financial sector to the government (if some kind of household debt forgiveness is mandated) will not work. Neither will the policy of forbearance, by which the government will not so much provide direct relief to the problem of overindebtedness as provide the conditions for some sort of healing to begin, through guarantees and fiscal stimulus, so that debt gets paid down gradually. In this case "forbearance" is a broad term that means an *indirect* government intervention in the economy's debt problems by attempting to restore health and therefore solvency through government spending rather than transference—a more direct approach of taking on the system's bad debts and then spreading debt forgiveness around like some sacred balm.

I have no confidence that either transference or forbearance will be enough to get us out of this crisis. Inflation, painful though it is, seems to be the only solution. The SuperCycle, as we will see, is at its core a process of disinflation that culminates in deflation; it necessarily implies indebtedness. We therefore reduce the debt overhang by *unraveling* the SuperCycle, which is to let go of our commitments to price stability—in other words, by creating inflation. But how do we do that? I argue that our central banks may have no choice but to behave "irresponsibly"—to stop talking the talk of price stability and to quietly monetize the debt on their books—that is, not withdraw the addition to the monetary base that central banks like the U.S. Fed and the Bank of England have recently undertaken and allow this to flow into the broader money supply, thus stoking inflation. Think of it as a noble lie: technically simple, but politically very difficult.

None of us wishes to get sucked into an inflation whirlwind. I argue that the way we will fight our way out of this coming era of superinflation with price rises in the double digits—if not hyperinflation where inflation is over 100 percent per year or possibly even stagflation where high inflation coexists with low growth—is by embracing a new monetary standard. It could mean a return to the Gold Standard or some other kind of bullion-backed system. Or perhaps even a new kind of monetary economics that emerges from a new kind of macroeconomics that resists the easy temptations of a naive reductionism— what equilibrium economists call "microfoundations" where the economy is assumed to behave like a rational individual, constantly impounding new information and seeking the most efficient course and striving to coming as close as possible to its aggregate goals—will point the way out.

These microfoundations are an economist's fetish. It took a century for economists to stop thinking in terms of constant returns to scale where output is directly proportional to the input. In the same way, many macroeconomists now are having a hard time relinquishing the idea that the aggregate economy is nothing more than an individual writ large. They have been slow to recognize that fallacies of composition are rife in this sort of thinking. They forgot the Keynesian paradox of thrift—where the individual's virtuous behavior of saving is likely to result in an even greater downturn. Now Keynes's idea is back and so are other equally pernicious kinds of paradoxes: the whole issue of counterparty risk is another fallacy of composition, where each individual institution's wish to limit risk for itself only increases the danger of collapsing the whole system. But I go much further in my criticism. I suggest in Chapter 2—but only suggest because doing any more than that would take me outside the scope of this book—that we look at the notion of macrocausality—where macroforces determine individual economic behavior rather than the other way around—as an alternative organizing principle for understanding the world economy.

DID OTHERS GET HERE FIRST?

Over the years, I have been asked by people with whom I have discussed these ideas how this theory is different from the Marxian or Kondratieffian way of analyzing capitalist economies. Both of these schools of thought argue that history has a direction and that economic factors are decisive in setting that direction. The modern Marxian explanation—best represented in the work of Robert Brenner of UCLA,[1] which I draw on in no small measure in Section III—is to argue that capitalist development is not cyclical (or supercyclical in this case) at all but has an in-built tendency toward overproduction. In this respect, Brenner's work is impressive. He has meticulously marshaled evidence showing that companies strive to maintain their *level* of profits even as their unit profit *margins* shrink in the face of increasing competition. This has produced a glut of production in certain sectors of the economy, notably manufacturing, where global competition is intense. But as I argue in Sections III and IV, manufacturing is just one flourish on a much larger pattern. Yes, the Modern SuperCycle did foster significant overcapacity in the production of manufactured goods, but an unwinding of capacity has been going on in a staggered fashion since the Japanese economy stumbled in the early 1990s. Our exchange rate system of flexible rates has drawn out the crisis in the global manufacturing sector far longer than it would have been under an exchange rate system of fixed rates like the Gold Standard. The recent boom in services and the attendant expansion of household balance sheets in the United States and elsewhere—along with the immense boost given to housing, that nontradable manufacturing industry[2]—cannot be convincingly explained by the Marxian theory of overproduction and its emphasis on shrinking profit margins.

The Kondratieff theory of long waves, on the other hand, has a meretricious quality about it. It seems to resurface during periods of crisis, and it has the appealing but elusive feature of seeming to explain some of the symptoms of the crisis—periods of deflation or inflation, asset accumulation, and so on—but then it seems to overreach in its explanation of the causal factors as well as many of the noneconomic effects. Kondratieff argued that the waves are triggered by the bunching together of product innovations from all sides of the economy, and that this in turn produces changes in methods of organization and process. The wave gathers speed and force as these changes build on each other, but it then begins to weaken as possibilities from those initial spurs are exhausted. The rest of his theory is really about the social and political changes that accompany these waves. So, for instance, it divides its approximately 50-year cycles into four "seasons," with very precise longevities: 25 years of income growth followed by high savings, then up to 5 years of a severe recession and asset deaccumulation, then 10 years of strong consumption during a mature phase of the economy, and finally an 18-year depression of which 15 years are spent in deflation. Overlaid on all this is an attempt to explain wars, famines, changes in social structures, and system-induced climate change—all in all, reminiscent of those sweeping Russian novels of the nineteenth century in which the sheer breadth and ambition of the narrative keeps you engrossed. But it is not what I would call a scientific theory that one could get one's arms around. The theory of the SuperCycle I put forth in the book gives no quarter to things like technology or innovation shocks. Everything here is endogenous—that is, can be explained by the actions of economic agents, whether they are central banks or the individual producer or consumer, in response to rising or falling inflation. At its core my framework is a simple one, but the implications are far-reaching.

ARE WE AT ONE OF HISTORY'S WATERSHED POINTS?

I am not so naive as to believe that the world will change all at once, nor do I believe that the way we have done things recently with such exuberance will simply disappear. I fully expect the business of finance and investments to continue, though somewhat constrained. We may retreat from the Market State, but we are unlikely to move back to a Welfare State. Even if the worst of my three scenarios—a grinding deflationary spell (the other scenarios being high inflation and stagflation)—should occur, there is little appetite and even fewer resources for an entitlement-based society today.

What could happen is that a prolonged malaise, a fever that refuses to break, the hope for a return to something recognizably normal in the economies most affected by this crisis swells and then is dashed repeatedly, could promote a search for a new political economy. Something like a Mutual State that functions around a decentralized financial system could then transpire from the wreckage of the Market State.[3] In the Mutual State, the Rube Goldberg–like financial system that we have so carelessly built makes way for something simpler, cleaner, closer to our needs, and less alienated from our wealth-producing activities. I use the word "mutual" because in this new state, each of us will have a stake in the outcome. At this stage in history, alas, it can only remain a distant hope.

A word about financialization is in order here. This theme recurs in the tableau of the Modern SuperCycle. It is a subtle idea—that the financial markets are a gigantic decision filter through which our plans and preferences for the present and future are run. In essence, an economic value (a price) can then be assigned to these preferences and they will be made tradable, giving us the pieces to put the jigsaw puzzle of our economic lives together. Somewhat provocatively, I present it in the book as our era's version of Fordism, that great economic and social phenomenon that defined the post–World War I business landscape and capped the achievements of the Progressive Era. Although Fordism, with its pledge of a mutually dependent relationship between employer and employee (by which the Ford Motor Company paid its employees much higher wages than the average because it saw them not only as workers but also as customers), survived the brutal contortions of the Great Depression, it came out of that period much diminished. Hopes that it would become the corporatist model for promoting stability and welfare without government intervention were shattered.

Financialization, on the face of it, could not be more different— after all, it celebrated the qualities of self-aggrandizement. Like Fordism in its heyday, though, it offered a promise of stability; but unlike Fordism, it does this through the spontaneous ordering of our collective preferences and actions filtered by the market rather than by the heroic efforts of individuals like Henry Ford. Both theories were therefore a search for a more efficient order—in one case detected by the rational observer, in the other created by brute force and will. And like Fordism after the Great Depression, financialization will not recover from this crisis.

So while I am convinced the era of financialization is over, I am quite confident that the practice of finance and financial innovation is here to stay. This is not a contradiction. Financialization is subscribed to by the leading central banks of the world in general and by the U.S. Federal Reserve in particular, where the complexity of financial markets is a *necessary* condition for achieving efficient equilibrium outcomes in creating wealth and where complex financial products are indispensable to households' attempts to smooth their consumption and saving decisions over the long term. Financial innovation, on the other hand, can be, and is, an advance that offers benefits that are tangible and are not based on casuistry. In effect, I am asking for a retreat from complex "Newtonian" finance and a return to simplified "Euclidean" finance.

In recognition of that, I have cast my mind ahead to the three scenarios that we face—a grinding deflation, high inflation, and stagflation—and how an investor can build a portfolio of assets in each of those very different circumstances. We will not face the Second Great Depression; more likely we will face the first Great Global Malaise—where the whole world looks like Japan—or perhaps the Great Stagflation. The sooner we grapple with the possibilities that the SuperCycle puts before us, the less we will have to complain about when the future gets here.

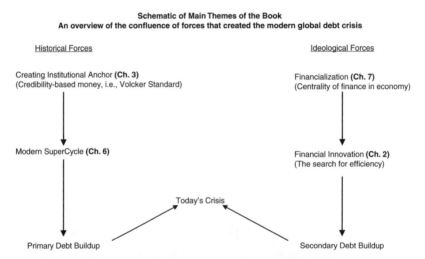

Schematic of Main Themes of the Book
An overview of the confluence of forces that created the modern global debt crisis

Historical Forces

Ideological Forces

Creating Institutional Anchor **(Ch. 3)**
(Credibility-based money, i.e., Volcker Standard)

Financialization **(Ch. 7)**
(Centrality of finance in economy)

Modern SuperCycle **(Ch. 6)**

Financial Innovation **(Ch. 2)**
(The search for efficiency)

Today's Crisis

Primary Debt Buildup

Secondary Debt Buildup

Primary Debt Buildup: Increased leverage in system, which is the result of terms-of-trade shocks from the SuperCycle.
Secondary Debt Buildup: Increased leverage in system, which is the result of financial innovation.

SuperCycles

Flaws in the Foundation

The aspects of things that are most important for us are hidden because of their simplicity and familiarity. (One is unable to notice something because it is always before one's eyes.) The real foundations of his enquiry do not strike a person at all. And this means we fail to be struck by what, once seen, is most striking and most powerful.

—LUDWIG WITTGENSTEIN,
Philosophical Investigations, Number 129

CHAPTER 1

The Elusive Science

Macroeconomics is riddled with fetishes. It has a spontaneous order fetish in its underlying philosophy where natural laws, no different from the laws of mechanics that determine the nature and movement of physical objects, govern our self-interested economic behavior to produce a collective outcome that is efficient if not always harmonious. Then there is an engineering fetish where monetary policy guides the economy to an optimal path and sets up a system to correct deviations from that path. This infatuation with the nineteenth-century science paradigms of the physical sciences has been our undoing because it has concealed the uncomfortable truth that macroeconomics fails the primary test of any modern science: it lacks predictive power, and, still more shockingly, it evades the unforgiving criterion of falsifiability. We will remain vulnerable to macroeconomics' failures until we take down the scaffolding and dismantle the structure of this false science. And since macroeconomists' theories are too important for merely scoring debating points—economists are, as Keynes said, the trustees of the possibility *of civilization—the rebuilding of macroeconomics itself needs to commence with haste.*

FINANCE'S PRIVILEGED POSITION IN THE MODERN ECONOMY

In 1990, upon seeing his country's economy begin its long slide into stagnation, Makoto Itoh, the great Japanese economist, wrote: "Capitalism seems to be running the film of history backwards by melting down the sustained trend of a century and returning to the older stage of liberalism. . . . [T]he reduction of the roles of the state and of trade unions with lighter industrial technologies makes capitalism in our age resemble capitalism in that earlier age."[1]

Such words were not taken seriously anywhere at the time they were written, least of all in the groves of American academe, where ideas profoundly hostile to those of Itoh and other unorthodox economists had long fertilized, incubated, and hatched. The financial firestorm that began in 2007, and that we are still struggling to contain, is a direct consequence of those ideas.

The intellectual origins of this crisis are there for all to see. Yet the surprising fact is that they remain invisible to many of our most intelligent policymakers and economic commentators who have observed the events unfold at close quarters. Is it a case of preferring to fail by conventional means rather than succeed by unconventional ones, as Keynes once put it, or is it a cognitive blindness that Wittgenstein seemed to detect in so many of our thinkers?

Suffice it to say that until many of the practices and institutions of modern finance are uprooted and regrafted, we will be condemned to relive these crises with increasing frequency and with more disruptive effects each time, or we must reconcile ourselves to an economy made sluggish by the unredeemed sins of the past. The image of W. B. Yeats's rough beast "with a gaze blank and pitiless as the sun . . . moving its slow thighs" comes to mind here.

In this section I will argue that while the constitution of modern finance is such that changing the way it functions in modern capitalism would be difficult if not impossible, the current crisis, by its sheer severity, should eventually succeed in producing a major shift. The foundations of asset pricing—and its astonishingly central role in what I shall refer to frequently in this book as the New Equilibrium Economics (NEE), a macroeconomic theory that has dominated universities, central banks, and multilateral financial institutions for much of the last quarter century—have cracked, and the edifice is being supported by a stubborn refusal to change.[2] We will achieve very little if we fail to eliminate this noxious theory and its many fetishes from our conventional habits of thinking and replace it with one from which will emerge a new—or perhaps even an older but certainly simpler and more intuitive—way of establishing the role of finance in our capitalist processes.

Meanwhile there is the politics of change. Economists from different generations and as far apart in theoretical bent as Axel Leijonhufvud, professor emeritus at UCLA, and Simon Johnson, former economic counselor at the International Monetary Fund (IMF), have commented on the extraordinary sight that has greeted their eyes: the full sinews of the U.S. government and its agencies exerting themselves to hold up a massive and broken system. What has shocked these two astute and wise observers of the global economy is that the efforts of the authorities have gone far beyond the necessary and now verge on the corrupt. Johnson's frequent use of the term "oligarchs" and Leijonhufvud's use of the word "oligopolies" betray their outrage at the turn of events. Let's hear it in the words of the one who may have been involved in fewer crises (since he did not spend any time at the IMF) but who was among the first to warn us of the bastardization of Keynes's General Theory in the 1960s and was among the earliest to see this crisis for what it really is, namely, a crisis of political economy:

> With the demise of Glass-Steagall fell the last bastion of Western populist opposition to the concentration of moneyed power in New York. The banking mergers of recent years have increased this concentration tremendously, and the political as well as economic power wielded by Wall Street is more palpable than ever. The Greenspan carry-trade years enriched these institutions and the people running them greatly. Nowhere has the upper tail of the income distribution been extended as far as in the financial industry. . . . The objective of preventing a deviation-amplifying financial collapse would admittedly seem to be in the public interest. But when we find the government repeatedly aiding and abetting the collusion of these financial behemoths, which we have allowed to become too big to fail, a rethinking of the relationship between government and big finance would seem to be in order.—Axel Leijonhufvud[3]

These financial institutions play the same role in our global economy as the country of, say, North Korea or, as some would even venture to say, even more worryingly, as Pakistan does in the international security system; in both cases we have come to dread the consequences of their falling apart. And if they know that we fear their collapse, will they not manipulate us to get what they want? Both Leijonhufvud and Johnson have made it clear that the age of moral hazard—those years of deregulation and the U.S. Congress's being at the service of Wall Street—will not be left behind until the U.S. Federal Reserve and the U.S. Treasury are rinsed clean of their ideological bias that the financial markets are much more than a place where the supply and demand for credit meet, but are indeed necessary conditions for all economic agents to efficiently bridge the present to the future, the requirement for economic stability.

The U.S. Fed, in particular, sees its relationship with deregulated financial markets as being the same as that of a falconer and his predator bird. The essence of falconry—to catch, kill, and retrieve—is frustrated if the falcon is maimed. The bird is an extension of the falconer's capacity in the act of hunting; the relationship is almost symbiotic. The financial markets are in the same way an extension of the Fed. They will follow the central bank's directives as long as their meaning is communicated well. And while certain other central banks—the Reserve Bank of New Zealand, the Banco Central do Brasil, and the German Bundesbank come to mind here—may have been more rigorous in the application of their own monetary policy rules, none of them has shown the inclination of the Fed to require the unfettered functioning of financial markets as central to its own mission. I shall have more to say about this later in this chapter after we have taken full measure of the conceptual framework that places finance so high in the hierarchy of activities that constitute the market-based capitalist economy.

THE UNFALSIFIABILITY OF ECONOMICS

In a recent essay Harvard economist N. Gregory Mankiw criticizes the current state of macroeconomics and invites a riposte from an equally distinguished macroeconomist, Michael Woodford of Columbia University.[4] Mankiw argues that since the rational expectations revolution in the 1970s—when economists cemented the central importance of self-correcting expectations in decision making at the level of each agent in the economy—too much stress has been placed on the development of macroeconomics as a science (with clear conceptual foundations) and too little on macroeconomics as a branch of engineering (an instructions manual for solving practical problems facing policymakers). As a result, he goes on to say, the emphasis on macroeconomic concepts and their internal consistency has "had little impact on practical macroeconomists" who work for or advise government departments and agencies. None of the recent advances in academic macroeconomics has been particularly useful in a practical manner. Because of this, Mankiw argues, policymakers depend on outdated macroeconomic theories to construct their models. Today's policy analysis, Mankiw says, appears to have descended from the work of Lawrence Klein and Franco Modigliani—models with hundreds of equations that do not include behavioral features. Mankiw is criticizing recent academic work in macroeconomics for being insufficiently pliable for policy use, leaving policymakers with little choice but to turn to obsolete formulations of the economy.

That Mankiw instead wishes for economists to become more like engineers reminds me of that doyenne of Cambridge Economics, the late Joan Robinson, whose comment on the peculiar fondness of American Keynesians—or pre-Keynesians as she would call them—for wanting to turn all of economics into a branch of engineering now rings so true. Had she lived a few more years, I can easily picture her speechless with anger at how macroeconomics has been turned into a vast graveyard for useless applications of industrial engineering, with the theory's frequent use of optimal control methods, as we shall see later in former Fed Governor Frederic Mishkin's comments on monetary policy.

A year after Mankiw's essay, Woodford presented his rejoinder, "Elements of a New Synthesis," at the 2008 Annual Meeting of the American Economic Association.[5] The rejoinder is a defense of current policy analysis and formulation—at least against Mankiw's claim that it fails to include recent thinking from the dominant Neoclassical Synthesis school of thought, which as mentioned previously I prefer to call the New Equilibrium Economics (NEE). Woodford's objective is to show the "reduced level of dissension within the field." He then catalogs the intellectual pedigree of each of the macroeconometric models used by the IMF, the Riksbank (Sweden's central bank), the Norges Bank (Norway's central bank), the European Central Bank (ECB), and, of course, the U.S. Federal Reserve. Toward the end, he cites then–Federal Reserve Governor Frederic Mishkin's speech to MIT's Undergraduate Economics Association in 2007 with its multiple references to optimal control theory, which is how to determine the optimal path of monetary policy in an environment where policy instruments are blown off course by unanticipated shocks, as if to rest his case that Mankiw's argument that economists need to become more like engineers is without merit.[6]

Yet I am sympathetic to at least the avowed aim of Mankiw's article—namely, that policymakers are lacking a set of tools that will help prepare them for the sort of seismic events that we have just come through. The conceptual framework that Mankiw found in its present form so intractable to the activity of problem solving has been turned into a rich vein of practical knowledge, if we are to be convinced by Woodford's citation of the many macroeconometric models in use throughout global banks. But we should remember that Woodford's answer to Mankiw's worries came in early 2008, just as the recent crisis had got under way but before the full scope and severity was felt. Woodford could confidently reel off the uses of modern theories in central bank models for price setting and expectations formation, but where did any of that help us when the global financial system began to fold in on itself a few months later?

Ever since Keynes wished for the day when economists would learn to regard themselves on par with dentists, engaged in modest but socially valuable activities of putting people out of discomfort, there has been a tendency for economists to emphasize the practical aspects of their training. But Keynes's dream sprang from the idea that the discovery of a robust theory would in turn yield methods to thwart the self-feeding spirals that capitalist economies were periodically prone to (and so protect society from the destructive effects of its own excesses); thus, economists would settle down into the humdrum existence of the journeyman. But those excesses—or rather, the predisposition toward those excesses—have not been wrung out of our economic system, not even with the sudden near collapse of the financial system that we have confronted in recent years. And so those methods that will forestall crises of this sort are still eluding us, and Keynes's wish cannot be satisfied just yet.

Mankiw implies in his article that modern macroeconomics is rich in concepts, each ripe with explanatory promise. So let's devote our efforts to writing an instructions manual for the central bankers or for those advising central bankers. My question is: can we? What is the predictive power of these concepts? Even in the crudely positivistic sense in which Milton Friedman made the case for economics in his classic essays,[7] where as long as there was a *correspondence* between predictions and events—and even if it turned out that the "black box" from where the predictions emanated was little more than an abracadabra machine—there should be no need for any doubt. In precisely that naive sense as well, modern macroeconomics, the NEE, has failed us. Recent events in the global economy and the inability of so much of model-driven work of the central banks to make sense of—let alone control—those events should have made that amply clear.

Friedman's simpleminded approach to asserting the value of economics—saying that it was a science in the face of criticism from those who argued that its models were built on unrealistic assumptions of perfect competition—worked rather well as a rhetorical device as long as economics was not facing questions about its real worth. Today it is, among a handful of influential economic journalists, commentators, policymakers, and even a few economists. Yet for all the handwringing that has taken place in public, the members of the economics profession that are actively involved in guiding policymakers seem strangely quiet about the ineffectiveness of their work. Could it be that they are stricken by an intellectual paralysis? In my opinion— and I shall spend much of the rest of the chapter reaching this conclusion—the NEE, the standard canon of macroeconomic thinking on which the central banks of the world build their forecasts and construct their scenarios, is unfalsifiable. This means the theories of modern macroeconomics have no built-in mechanism that signals that the theory is wrong. Little can be predicted correctly, but everything is sought to be explained.

Let's unpack that a bit. For a theory to be falsifiable, it needs, first, to stick its neck out and say that given the following conditions, we expect Event *A* will occur. But that is not enough because, if this is all it offered, it would be the same as Friedman's positivist theory of correspondence and modern macroeconomics would have failed the Friedman test in every major crisis the global economy has faced in the last 25 years. Instead, the theory needs to go further; it must also say that given the following conditions, if Event *B* (or *C* or *D*) occurred, the theory will be proved wrong. This is the strong definition of *falsifiability*, and all robust scientific theories must demonstrate this falsifiability. A theory that cannot point to events that will prove it wrong is considered unfalsifiable.

By these measures, the New Equilibrium Economics is not a robust scientific theory. As in George Orwell's memorable metaphor of lifeless English, it is like the soft snow that falls on facts, covering all the details and blurring all the outlines. We are living through an economic convulsion that will leave deep rutted tracks in the global economy, and yet our body of macroeconomic thought has nothing meaningful to say about these events because it has neither the ability to predict nor to satisfactorily explain.

For instance, the American Economic Association's annual meeting in January 2008 had organized a series of papers to be presented on macroeconomics that came under the rubric "Convergence in Macroeconomics." Even as gale force winds were tearing up the global financial markets, the symposium's main paper was devoted to explaining the Great Moderation— the name given to the absence of macroeconomic volatility in the U.S. economy in recent history. Another was on why none of the canonical theories of NEE were yet ready for prime time since "some of its shocks and other features were not structural or consistent with micro evidence," which is just a technical way of saying that the shocks that hit the economy in the models are not consistent with the behavior of the representative agent in the same models and that more work needs to be done to achieve the desired consistency.[8] The orthodoxy of modern macroeconomics is a hall of mirrors; yet it is still being applied inside central banks and policymaking institutions.

THEORETICAL PHYSICS AS A CASE STUDY

But could the current state of economics represent the pitch of night before the dawn? Ask modern physicists—who have had the spotlight on them longer than any of the other theorists— and they will offer examples of crises that were eventually overcome. One such dramatic period occurred at the beginning of the twentieth century. The discoveries of X rays, electrons, protons, and other forms of radiation emitted from atoms had strained classical physics to the breaking point; so had experiments on light, which posed a challenge to long-accepted notions of space and time.

In 1904 luminaries of the scientific world gathered at the Congress of Arts and Science in St. Louis, Missouri, to discuss the plight of physics. At the meeting, Ernest Rutherford, Henri

Poincaré, Ludwig Boltzmann, and other leading lights outlined the conundrums they faced and suggested possible resolutions. Chen Ning Yang of the State University of New York, and Nobel Laureate 1957 for his experimental work on the existence of a subtle asymmetry in particle interactions, wrote in volume 5 of the American Institute of Physics' History of Modern Physics series: "They all recognized there was a great crisis; . . . they lamented that everything they thought they understood was wrong."

Yet before the year was out, Einstein had formulated his theory of special relativity, which resolved the paradoxes posed by the propagation of light with startling new conceptions of time and space. Two decades later quantum mechanics had been discovered, which provided a strange but accurate description of the behavior of atoms.

In an interview in 1994, Dr. Yang compared the crisis of 1904 with the intellectual doubts that were plaguing contemporary theoretical physicists, who were searching for a mathematical principle to reconcile the contradictory results of relativity and quantum mechanics.[9] This more recent project in theoretical physics—known as *superstring theory*—required looking for some great advance in mathematics to resolve the incompatibility between the two kinds of phenomena, rather than being guided by evidence from the physical world. This, he worried, was a kind of regress, and he warned that it spoke of an intellectual exhaustion in the research program.

What would Dr. Yang make of NEE as the dominant paradigm in macroeconomics? He would be close to despair. As the dominant theory, NEE has remained strangely oblivious to all the crises that have brought the world crashing around it. Nor is anything expected of it, even more surprisingly. Even the recent highly publicized admission by former Fed Chairman Alan Greenspan that he had found a flaw ("Yes, I've found a flaw. . . . I don't know how significant or permanent it is. But

I've been very distressed by that fact. . . . A flaw in the model that I perceived is the critical functioning structure that defines how the world works"[10]) provoked no soul searching about the validity of the underlying theory. The *cri de coeur* from the former head of the U.S. central bank has been consigned by his successor, Ben Bernanke, and that new breed of entrepreneur of ideas (exemplified by Frederic Mishkin of Columbia University who between policymaking and academic roles has also been a consultant to the governments of Ecuador and Iceland on the liberalization of their domestic financial systems) who emerge from their rabbits' warren of offices in universities and central banks at such times, into the now overflowing category of general but inconsequential criticisms of the free market system. These are the Defenders of the True Faith—and we will be hearing more from them in the course of the book.

CAUSAL AND ONTOLOGICAL STATEMENTS

But, as asked earlier, do the underlying propositions of NEE not just stand up to the rigors of evidence but also demonstrate that they are falsifiable? And what is the NEE—or any theory, for that matter—worth if it is not falsifiable?

The theory cannot be tautological. It should be more than a body of *trivially true causal statements* about the world. A good illustration of these self-evident truths is the statement "All fires in this town are caused by flammable material." Such a statement is necessarily true—since the definition of *flammable* is "being able to catch fire"—but trivially so. It doesn't enlighten us about the workings of the world, and it doesn't persuade people to change their ways, unless we wish to ban cloth, wood, and paper from all homes and force people to write on stone slates and live in glass houses. On the other hand, the statement "All fires in this town are caused by arsonists" is falsifiable. But if we later find a loose electrical connection or a faulty circuit box or evidence of a lightning strike on a certain house, we can ascertain the statement's truth value. And if we cannot find any of those other causes, then the hypothesis is acceptable until we find refuting evidence. According to this view, truth is always conditional because tomorrow it could be falsified.

And then there are *ontological statements* about the world, which do not establish any cause and effect but are simply statements of fact—or more precisely, statements of the existence or nonexistence of something. Here falsifiability has its own subtlety. How does one falsify the existence of something? For instance, if the statement to be falsified is "*A* exists," one does this by establishing the nonexistence of *A*. How does one do that?

It might help to take a concrete example. Take the case of the Bush administration's assertion that weapons of mass destruction (WMDs) were to be found in Iraq. An ultimatum was delivered to the Ba'athist regime in Iraq that it would have to prove the WMDs did not exist. The regime thus had to establish the nonexistence of WMDs. How would it do that? It could have the U.N. inspectors—and later the U.S. Army inspectors, which were given more time—search for the offending items. Since Iraq had precise territorial boundaries that demarcated an area that could be thoroughly searched, not finding the weapons would have implied their nonexistence. But this was not incontrovertible. Despite the exhaustive search that lasted several months that failed to turn up the weapons, many American conservatives continued to argue that the weapons were ferreted across the border to Syria, Iran, or some third place. The set of possibilities was now no longer limited by the territorial boundaries of Iraq.

In this way certain ontological statements—notably those that require us to establish the nonexistence of something—are not falsifiable in the strict sense that it is possible to produce evidence that disproves the hypothesis. This occurs when the set of possibilities is open and infinite.

You are probably asking: what does this have to do with New Equilibrium Economics? As you will see when I sketch its outlines, like all scientific theories, NEE claims validity until it is falsified. But NEE's central statements cannot be falsified since they are either tautological causal propositions or the set of possibilities to establish the nonexistence of something is unlimited. Specifically, critics must demonstrate that the world we live in approximates the world described in the NEE. If the "real" world is different from the world described by the theory, then the theory claims it is still valid. In other words, the world must conform to the structure of the theory rather than the other way around.

And in a manner of speaking, this is the frustration that Mankiw is expressing as well. Though he may see nothing philosophically (or, rather, methodologically) wrong with a theory that is waiting for the real world to come to it rather than for it to go out and work with the facts the world throws at it, at least he wishes to be given the tools, no matter how imperfect, that will help him tinker with things when the world risks going off the rails.

So let us get to this theory, to the fetishistic notion of spontaneous order that animates it, and then to the role of this human activity called "finance" that is given such pride of place in NEE economists' whole scheme. The words of Frederic Mishkin, at the time a governor of the U.S. Federal Reserve, sets the scene for us when he called finance the brain of the economy: "That is, it acts as a coordinating mechanism that allocates capital, the lifeblood of economic activity, to its most productive uses by businesses and households. If capital goes to the wrong uses or does not flow at all, the economy will operate inefficiently, and ultimately economic growth will be low. No work ethic can compensate for a misallocation of capital and the resulting failure to invest in the most profitable ventures."[11]

ARCHAEOLOGY OF MACROECONOMIC IDEAS

The story of macroeconomics begins with the mercantilists, a group of economists who held that a nation should aim at an excess of exports over imports and so at accumulating bullion (purchasing power in the form of precious metals). This approach dominated economic thought for two and a half centuries beginning in the early sixteenth century. The mercantilist idea is rooted in the concept of trade. It is associated with a multiplicity of economic systems, each endowed with particular resources or products, who try to gain advantage through exchange. This is an interesting problem in and of itself because we find ourselves working out how to make the best use of what is already available; that is, how to redistribute resources so as to achieve the best allocation in line with the preferences of those who participate in these systems.

We may envisage a state of affairs in which each of the economic systems has reached an *internal* equilibrium, internal only because the economic systems do not trade among themselves. However, once they begin to trade with each other it is easy to show that this change from no trade to trade should bring gains for all. Working out the best final allocation of resources, when preferences and endowments between them are different, becomes a problem of rationality. That is to say, if each agent is responding to what is best for him or her, there should be an allocation of resources that is attainable through exchange such that it maximizes utility, satisfaction, welfare, or any variant of that ideal.

The impact of the benefits of trade (or exchange) cast a powerful spell on the minds of those early mercantilist economists. The mercantilists lacked the appropriate analytical methods to support their intuition about the importance of worldwide trade. Such a theory would have to wait until much later when the Marginalist revolution—led by Alfred Marshall and Stanley

Jevons and developed still further by F. Y. Edgeworth and Leon Walras—got under way. These economists in turn set the foundations for the early work in Equilibrium Economics.

In the meantime, we had the classical theorists such as Adam Smith, David Ricardo, and Thomas Malthus, whose overriding goal was to describe the production of wealth, and its distribution, inside a self-perpetuating system. Here the ownership of the means of production became critical to capturing the surplus generated by economic activity.

On the heels of the classical economists arrived the first equilibrium economists (or the first "equilibriumists"). Breaking with the classical tradition (see Figure 1.1), the equilibriumists went back to the mercantilist conception of wealth as a set of endowments of scarce resources that could be rationalized—that is, made better through exchange—and then they placed that conception at the very center of their scheme. But, with the equilibriumists, we got a picture not of a dynamic society but of a static one where wealth existed in various forms and needed to be exchanged in a way so that society's welfare could increase. By the mid–twentieth century this theory was extended to describing the behavior of the economy as a whole by working out the optimal behavior of each economic agent that made up this economy and then looking for where exchange between them was possible. The next step was to accommodate a large number of different goods and diverse preferences of individuals. The goal of the equilibriumists was to see that a *general* equilibrium existed—that is, where each individual bought and sold the optimal quantities given of all goods and the total supply of each good was equal to the total demand for it. Over the years, this simple idea of a system of exchange was refined from a static model to a dynamic model by introducing many time periods into the decision-making process. This newly dynamic model is known as the renowned Arrow-Debreu equilibrium conditions.

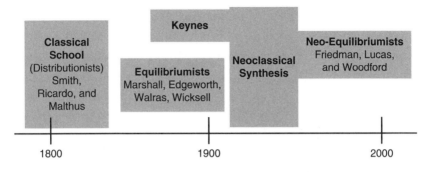

FIGURE **1.1 Archaeology of Macroeconomics**

ENTER FINANCIAL MARKETS

But for the purposes of our story we take a huge leap forward to the late 1960s and the 1970s when two American economists, Jack Hirshleifer and Roy Radner (called H-R from here on), introduced financial markets into the existing equilibrium model to do two things:

A. To find a way to bridge the consumption and saving plans of individuals between present and future

B. Related to A, to enable economic agents to insure against uncertainty about the future

These economic agents—whether households or firms—are described as seeking to maximize at every instant the present value of their current and future welfare in accordance with their preferences and subject to the obvious constraints of income, wealth, and information.

To understand the model, it is essential that the reader understand the importance given to information in the NEE. Most of us regard uncertainty as endemic to our lives. It plagues our decision making. But prior to H-R, uncertainty showed up in the work of the equilibrium economists as an information problem. In the idealized world of the early Equilibrium Economics,

we have all the information we need—and it is correct information. And since each of us knows what others in the system
know, there is also no room for coordination problems—where
my actions spill over and impair your actions in some way. This
was known as "having perfect information" because each economic agent has perfect foresight. Hence uncertainty is elimi-
nated. The H-R model, though, inserts uncertainty into the
equilibrium model, which is how financial markets enter it.

To better understand H-R's handling of the information
problem and thus the need for financial markets, let us step
back and examine how the bridging between the present and
the future takes place. This bridging can happen only if we pos-
sess the means to transfer today's income for tomorrow's use,
or tomorrow's expected income for today's use—what economists sometimes call the intertemporal allocation of resources.
These transfers are made possible by holding financial assets
as a way of storing our savings. Or if we wish to go the other
way and bring the future's resources to bear on us today, we
can borrow against future receipts. Sometimes we may wish to
do a bit of both, buying assets as a repository for our savings
and then borrowing in part or whole against those assets if the
need should so arise. We can make the model still more complicated by buying an asset whose cost is greater than the savings
we put into it, and we can borrow the difference. (Today we
practitioners would call that "leverage"). All this shuffling of
today's and tomorrow's income and pushing assets back and
forth are ways of financial planning but are also ways of handling uncertainty.

Again, since the H-R model assumes a world of imperfect
information, financial markets also exist for economic agents
to engage in direct purchases or sales of "insurance" against
certain events' occurring; that is, they can take on or shed
risk in accordance with their preferences and their view of the
future. Financial markets are therefore not just necessary but

also central to the whole arrangement of exchange in New Equilibrium Economics.

Of course, all this presupposes that in the Hirshleifer-Radner model of the economy, each agent, in the course of planning for the future consistently with his or her preferences and views of the future, will be assigning probabilities to different outcomes, sometimes called *states of nature*. Each person has a certain view of the likelihood of what the world will look like at different points in time and what those states of nature mean for his or her plans for the future. Intuitively, we know that different people's different states of nature will ultimately be reflected in the prices of assets—including now various kinds of insurance contracts, which agents might wish to transact in order to optimize their plans.

Let's unpack this a little bit more. Having seen what the purpose of financial assets really is in the H-R model—first, as a way to bridge present and future and, second, as a form of insurance—each asset price can now be thought of as a combination of payoffs in different states of the world at different times expected by each individual. Markets are said to be *complete* when there are buyers and sellers whose expected payoffs in these states of nature bring them together to conduct a transaction. Markets are said to be *efficient* when there is no room for arbitrage—in other words, expected payoffs for identical states of nature would not be transacted at two different prices at the same instant. Prices need to be unique in efficient markets, which is to say there should be a one-to-one correspondence between expected payoffs and asset prices.

Let us take an example from the everyday world of commercial transactions: You need euros at the end of the month because your assessment of the state of the world requires you to be in that currency on a certain day. So you borrow in U.S. dollars today from your bank—paying a borrowing rate—and then convert that amount at today's exchange rate and invest it in a European bank for which you are paid a lending rate. At the end of the month you withdraw the funds in euros and use the proceeds for whatever you had in mind. The actual conversion rate, thus, would have been the principal and interest paid on the dollar borrowed amount equated to the principal and interest received on the euro deposit amount.

But rather than go through the rigmarole of this multistep process, it might be easier to contract to buy the same amount of euros at the end of the month in the forward foreign exchange market. And the net conversion rate should be exactly the same. The point is that this asset price—(the cost of euros against U.S. dollars) which is the payoff in some expected state of the world, one month hence, and which is obtainable two different ways, (a) by borrowing and depositing in two different currencies or (b) contracting in the forward FX market—should bring us to the same result. This is the no-arbitrage condition in asset pricing—in other words, it is an efficient market.

So let us say you are getting a better rate buying euros against U.S. dollars with the two-step process described above than with the one-step forward markets. Well, you can make riskless profits by selling euros forward and then delivering those euros using the two-step process.

Markets, then, are efficient when the no-arbitrage condition holds. Individuals and firms—economic agents more broadly—are able to purchase assets for every possible realization of all types of idiosyncratic shocks, and so they are able to hedge away these shocks. Only aggregate consumption shocks—which is to say those truly unexpected events that affect the consumption and saving plans for all economic agents, and so necessitate a change in all their plans and perturb the equilibrium—cannot be insured away. Specifically, these shocks upset the rate at which agents plan intertemporally. Consumption and saving decisions in the economy go awry; work and leisure decisions are severely disturbed; convergence of plans is severely threatened. Equilibrium becomes elusive. Markets become incomplete.

RECAPPING MAIN IDEAS

We saw the idea of trade achieve primacy with the mercantilists, then recede briefly when the classicals like Smith, Ricardo, and Malthus emphasized production at the expense of exchange, but then come roaring back to life with the equilibriumists like Marshall and Jevons, who looked at individual markets, and those like Edgeworth and Walras, who sought a more general equilibrium covering all markets. Finally we saw the rise of the new breed of equilibriumists (neo-equilibriumists) who introduced uncertainty and time, that is, present and future, into their general equilibrium theories—still with exchange as the basis of all improvement. Financial markets were now ensconced firmly on center stage.

THE KEYNESIAN TURN

But we have overlooked a detour in our story. A detour is all it turned out to be, though what a show it was as long as it lasted! I am talking about the Keynesian turn, of course. The sheer marvel of this part of the story was not only that it offered a clean solution to an unexpected failure of the system to correct itself, but like the Immaculate Conception, it didn't seem to have any ancestry. Keynes's theory eschewed individual markets and individual preferences. In fact, it eschewed everything that was unique to the individual household, the individual firm, the individual good, the individual market. In the framework he developed, aggregate quantities—such as aggregate consumption or aggregate investment—could produce really bad outcomes. It wasn't quite classical—it couldn't have been bothered with how the surplus was distributed—and yet it was avowedly, determinedly, nonequilibriumist. As stated earlier, it engaged in a high degree of aggregation, paying little notice to individual expectations, and when it did account for these expectations, it offered them as vague statements of fact not deserving of further attention. Individual expectations were there to solve a problem, which was that at times of crisis there is an insufficiency of effective (aggregate) demand, and liquidating supply to bring it in line with the lower demand only ends up lowering demand still further. Liquidationist policies, in other words, only set off a downward spiral where supply and demand chase each other into a bottomless depression.

The equilibriumists noticed that Keynes's style was to focus on the interdependence of the different aggregate variables. They explained that the indistinct form of a general equilibrium theory was struggling to get out from inside the slapdash aggregation of his work. They needed to usurp his theory and "reduce" it to the individual—individual expectations, individual preferences, and individual optimization. But first they needed to discredit the theory as it stood.

The opportunity came with the appearance of stagflation in the 1970s. Stagflation was seen as a dramatic empirical failure of Keynes's theory because the orthodox version, speaking in the language of aggregate variables, did not allow for this phenomenon. It simply did not countenance the possibility that weakness in output and rising inflation could coexist. It is worth pointing out that Keynesianism was falsifiable and so could at least claim to be a scientific theory.

Keynes's General Theory was presented by the equilibriumists as failing to take account of expectations. Expectations affect an individual's decisions. How could it be that governments take action to stimulate demand, and so raise output and wages, and yet businesses do nothing to raise prices, effectively pushing real wages back to their earlier level? And in turn reduce the supply of labor, causing output to drop as well? Should we not end up in a worse position than when we started, with the same level of output, higher nominal wages but higher prices and so the same level of real wages? The expectations of workers and businesses, it was argued—by the equilibriumists—are not static but are forward looking; individuals are always calculating rationally what is best for them and responding accordingly.

Whether there was more to the Keynesian revolution than solving the problem of insufficient demand is still the subject of heated exchanges, erupting every few decades. In the 1960s and 1970s a band of Keynesian true believers led by the redoubtable Joan Robinson turned Cambridge, England, into a bastion of resistance against anything to do with the U.S.-led equilibrium counterrevolution. They insisted in seeing in Keynes's work a whole new way of describing the economy that was closer to the classical approach of how much is produced, who decides that, and who gets what share of the spoils. The objections of the equilibriumists were just red herrings, they said; they were irrelevant because they were criticizing something Keynes never proposed.

More recently, a group of American "post-Keynesians" inspired by the late Hyman Minsky have used Keynes's inchoate views on asset prices to mount an attack on the efficient market hypothesis. Much has been written about these guerrilla wars, and I shall allude to them briefly, not to advance their cause but in fact to argue that they do not go far or deep enough.

THE MILITANT REACTION

In the 1980s, as memories of demand-led crunches faded but memories of inflation remained raw, there was a strong drive to rehabilitate the self-correcting qualities of a market economy. There was even a militant reaction led by the storm trooper division of the equilibriumists, known as the Real Business Cycle (RBC) theorists, who argued that shocks administered by technological changes do show up as profound changes in individuals' optimization of present and future plans, but these too would pass. It would be unwise to even try to stabilize the economy—that is, counter these forces with fiscal and monetary policies—because in the long run they would retard the self-correcting mechanism of the economy.

What was truly revolutionary (or perhaps truly reactionary because it reflected a return to mercantilist preoccupations with exchange) about the RBC school of thought was that it argued that money had no essential role to play in the economy, an idea which it called the "superneutrality of money." Because the RBC school held that intertemporal decisions of saving and consuming, investing and producing, did not require money—since they were plans—and that money enters the picture only as a medium of exchange and a unit of account, the presence of a monetary sector whose fluctuations would spill over and affect the real variables had no role to play. A core belief in the RBC system of thought is that equilibrium occurs, markets clear, quantities and prices are determined, and resources are allocated—all without granting money any role beyond that of a medium of exchange and a unit of account. Preferences and terms of substitution across time were all that mattered if it were not for technology-induced shocks.

Note, however, that the exclusion of money as anything other than a means of reducing friction in the pure exchange of signals among economic agents about their plans does not mean that finance is not indispensable to this way of thinking about the economy. The reader should remember, at the expense of repetition to the point of exhaustion, that *finance* is *not* synonymous with *money*, and the *financial sector* is not synonymous with the *monetary sector*. The financial sector provides assets and liabilities, which is how economic agents bridge the present to the future and manage risks and opportunities emanating from an uncertain future.

But the elimination of money as a balance that individuals would choose to hold for more than just transaction purposes did not square with experience either personal or institutional. Why did central banks exist? And not just exist but actually have influence—whether good or bad—on output and employment and prices? And didn't the large body of work done by Milton Friedman and Anna Schwartz—the keepers of the monetarist flame—confirm empirically that monetary influence, especially with regard to the Great Depression when the failure of the U.S. central bank to ease policy while the United States was on the Gold Standard, was the cause of the deepening downturn.

THE REVISIONISTS MAKE PEACE (AMONG THEMSELVES)

Eventually, a temporary truce was struck between these two reactionary schools within the NEE, and a synthesis emerged. The RBC model would hold with all its deep structural explanations, but it would include a role for money and for central banks. These central banks would be committed to controlling the supply of money so that the nominal rate would be zero. That was the price at which the government "created" money—in a paper money system at least. Inflation was not supposed to exist in the RBC world, but just in case it appeared anomalously, the central bank was there to expunge it. All other interest rates for all other maturities would be determined in line with people's plans for the future: the intertemporal rate of substituting future consumption for today's consumption. The yield curve would be nothing more or less than the rate at which agents would, on average, forsake today's consumption for tomorrow's, or that of six months hence, or 10 years, or 30 years.

Yet on a deeper intellectual level, something continued to nag. The RBC theorists were not able to account for the actual power of central banks to affect output, job creation, and inflation by controlling the money supply. Something must give money its effectiveness. The answer finally came to be found in the idea of "broken perfection." This is the name I give to the concept that forms the core of the NEE that infuses academic and policymaking thinking. In the academic world it goes by the name of New Keynesian Economics—think of it as a variation of the general body of theory that I have been calling the NEE—but there is nothing Keynesian about it. It was invented for one purpose only: to be an explanation for why money matters. Not surprisingly, it is embraced by central bankers everywhere.

AT LAST A DOMINANT PARADIGM

The New Keynesian explanation is at its heart the old RBC theory with its emphasis on complete (supplying every demand at a price) and efficient (no arbitrage) markets that always cleared except when there were exogenous shocks that temporarily perturbed preferences and so pushed the economy out of equilibrium until its self-correcting forces cranked up. But New Keynesianism also assumed that there were rigidities; that is, wages and prices were contractually set for certain lengths of time because it was rational for firms and individuals faced with uncertainty about prices and costs to do exactly that.

Hence, due to the presence of this sort of "stickiness," changes in the short-term nominal interest rates—which a central bank was able to control to a large extent by controlling the banking system's reserves and thereby control the amount of funds that reached the interbank market for short-term borrowing and lending—would not be accompanied by an instantaneous change in inflation. Inflation would lag changes in interest rates. Thus, *real* rates could be changed, and these variations would bring about changes in consumption and saving and, through them, changes in output and employment.

By adjusting real rates to stabilize the system as it is hit by exogenous shocks, the central bank achieves all sorts of political victories. It builds its reputation and achieves credibility. At some point its credibility would become so great that it would be able to use the short-term rate as an anchor—a signaling mechanism by which it would be telling economic agents where it wanted inflation to end up, which most would want as close to zero as possible. This is the holy grail of central banking: inflation targeting, not just because like a sorcerer it can magically realize inflation at exactly the level it desires but because by doing so, it is making its own action redundant. After all, the reason there are rigidities is because economic agents don't know what future inflation is, and so they do what is rational for them to do, namely, lock themselves into long-term contracts, which embeds inflation in the system.

But the uncertainty of inflation is a manufactured uncertainty. It exists because of insufficient information about each other's plans. If the central bank takes away this uncertainty because its power—derived from its credibility—allows it to do so, then the nominal rigidities will gradually disappear and we will be back to the RBC world of markets that will always clear other than when hit by exogenous shocks (see Figure 1.2).

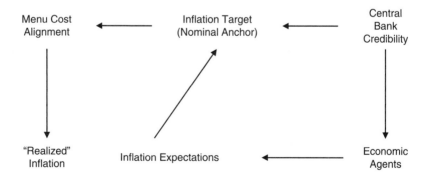

FIGURE **1.2 Central Bank as Maestro**

So we have come full circle now. The dominant paradigm of NEE is therefore one that talks of intertemporal optimization of plans of economic agents who come together to create complete and efficient markets with finance playing a critical—indeed indispensable—role in making this happen, both in smoothing consumption between present and future and in mitigating risk as perceived by households and firms. The monetary sector—represented by the central banks—also facilitates in the *perfecting* of these markets by earning credibility and producing a convergence of inflation expectations around a locus, and then finally through inflation targeting, which eliminates the rigidities that entrench inflation in the economy. The goal of the successful inflation-targeting central bank is thus to render itself extinct with its own success.

FROM PURE BLISS TO CRISIS, OR THE PERILS OF TOO MUCH SUCCESS

Even before we get to that long sought after but never attained state of pure bliss, a successful monetary policy can produce unwelcome and unintended consequences. This is how the housing bubble in the U.S. economy—and many other parts of the world—is explained away by the New Keynesian variant of the NEE.

In recent years, heightened risk tolerance was created and sustained by the environment of low volatility with respect to output and inflation. This is the aforementioned "Great Moderation" explanation of how asset booms occur as a consequence of central banks' being *too* successful in achieving their objectives. As a result, economic agents' intertemporal plans temporarily shift strongly toward present consumption and investment. Put another way, the success of the U.S. Fed in achieving price stability was instrumental in making people's expectations overshoot on the side of optimism—a sentiment that, we are told, was a *rational* response to the changed habitat of low volatility of inflation and output. And financial markets are there, innocent as always, only responding to these changed needs by providing the means for them to be satisfied through the most ingenious forms of financial innovation.

Let's have it in the words of that well-known spokesman for this dominant paradigm, Frederic Mishkin, at the Jackson Hole symposium on September 1, 2007. Mishkin said the recent experience with subprime loans fit a boom-bust pattern of financial innovation. Rapid financial change, triggered by innovation and deregulation, leads to a lending boom. This process, he said, deepens the financial system by matching the saving and investment needs of households and firms better, and it is "vital" for the economy in the long run. But, he continued, a lending boom can "outstrip the available information resources in the financial system, raising the odds of costly, unstable conditions in financial markets in the short run."[12]

So while systematic changes in monetary policy are generally accepted within the dominant paradigm as the most important determinant of the Great Moderation and of the asset booms that followed, a split has recently emerged over what caused the collapse of the housing boom and whether this too was a rational response to new information. This is an important debate because the split between the Real Business Cycle and the New Keynesian schools, the two key strains of thinking in the NEE, has reappeared after years of agreeable coexistence.

We have already heard from the main spokesman for the New Keynesians, Frederic Mishkin, who admits that monetary policy can have malignant effects but who also says that, on balance, monetary policy and financial markets form a powerful tag team. So monetary policy—an endogenous variable—administers the shock by confusing economic agents with its unexpected success, inducing them to make long-term shifts in their plans, while financial markets respond and asset bubbles form and then burst, causing widespread damage.

The RBC school meanwhile is having a hissy fit. They have gone back to arguing that asset prices react only to unexpected changes in aggregate consumption, which in turn is due to exogenous shifts in technology or preferences. The unforeseen effects of that endogenous thing called "monetary policy" were always meant to be temporary and not particularly severe. (These economists now say that while they agreed to accept the nonneutrality of money and conceded a degree of effectiveness to monetary policy, they did so with the clear understanding that policy would have temporary effects.) Yet this global economic crisis has been severe by any measure, and the housing boom that preceded it was also global in scope and distended values quite significantly, so something else must have caused it. Not surprisingly, RBC economists are arguing that something truly exogenous is at work here.

REVISITING FALSIFIABILITY AND THE NEE

Yet my point is that this debate between the two variants of the NEE (the RBC and the New Keynesians) is not a scientific debate in the sense that it falls prey to the unfalsifiability criterion that I mentioned earlier.

Let us consider each in turn. *Exogenous* is the technical term for something that cannot be accounted for inside the model; like a massive asteroid crashing into Earth, it comes out of nowhere. The overwhelming part of the RBC research program therefore assumes that there are these random shocks that hit the economy and that economic agents quickly adjust to them. Forcing individuals' plans to converge is not the desired goal. The RBC school would have little sympathy for Mankiw's appeal for a new toolkit and Woodford's response that the kit that exists is robust and is usable.

According to the RBC, the world economy was battered by a technology-induced or some other exogenous shock that triggered profound changes in our view of the world, necessitating deep adjustments in the rate at which we trade off today's consumption against that of the future, throwing financial markets out of equilibrium and making them incomplete. That is, buyers and sellers no longer had a marketplace to visit to transact their plans. More precisely, as economic agents' risk aversion rose on the back of these changes, financial markets were not able to provide agents with the means to insure themselves against the future, and so they fled to the safest and most liquid government bonds, shunning all other assets. Hence the rally in government bonds, and hence the strengthening of the Japanese yen and the U.S. dollar, as leveraged investors feared an unwind. These are investors who have for years borrowed in these two currencies and invested in assets in other, mostly emerging-market, currencies. This flight to home was not a flight to safety but was really a flight to a settling of accounts by lenders in those two currencies, and it led to the credit crunch and eventually our recent steep recession.

At one level, the effects described here are accurate. Many of these things did happen. But when we attribute them to some exogenous force, whether a slow-moving technology shock, or sunspots, or insidious electromagnetic waves that seep into our brains and make us change our consumption preferences for the present and the future, how do we establish the existence of the source of the shock in question?

Remember the falsifiability of ontological statements: we can disprove the existence of something only by *not* finding it and that would be possible only if we were dealing with a set of possibilities that was closed and finite. Since the RBC school does not tell us what sort of shock it is, only that it is exogenous, this becomes a wild goose chase, philosophically speaking. We cannot identify the shock.

Let us now examine the New Keynesian argument that traces the cause of the collapse to monetary policy's unforeseen and undesirable ability to move the economy out of equilibrium. Is it falsifiable? The shifting of intertemporal preferences—the changes that occur in aggregate to our plans for and expectations about the future—is not observable either. So here too we are back to the flight-to-safety and flight-to-home phenomena evidenced in the financial markets.

The response of many equilibriumists to the critique offered here would be: so what? What's wrong with regarding the flight phenomena as the starting point of our analysis that a shock, whether exogenous or the result of misreading endogenous monetary policy signals, is working its way through the economy? We don't need to see the actual shock any more than we need to see a black hole when our radio telescopes show us a planet being torn to shreds.

Now we have a causal, and not just an ontological, proposition to work with. This is how it goes: Shocks produce flight-to-safety phenomena, which indicate a crisis. How do we falsify this proposition? We cannot because it is a tautological statement, and therefore it is trivially true. It is analogous to my earlier "fire is caused by flammable material" proposition. This is why. All economic crises are identified by flight to safety or flight to home; the flight phenomenon does not establish what caused it. Therefore, it is quite possible that it has nothing to do with shifts in our preferences, and so the cause of that shift, whether an exogenous shock or a misreading of monetary signals, is a matter of speculation, not science. This is where today's prevailing macroeconomic theories break down and expose themselves as flawed—they do not predict nor do they explain the recent events in the global economy. As a result, the door is now wide open to some new, alternative interpretations of events that lie outside of the dominant models of macroeconomic behavior—in effect, new macroeconomic theories.

ALTERNATIVE INTERPRETATIONS

A compelling answer to the New Equilibrium Economics' failure to offer a convincing explanation or a convincing solution to our economic problems is to be found in the writings of the late Hyman Minsky and the Japanese-American economist Richard Koo. Both can be called post-Keynesians, a label that is reserved for economists who draw heavily on Keynes's theory yet distill a finely wrought interpretation of his work. But as deep and subtle as their work is in helping us understand this crisis in particular—how we got into it, in the case of Minsky; and how we get out of it, in the case of Koo—neither can marshal anything like the sort of resources needed to take on the NEE. Minsky and Koo can best be described as using slingshots unleashed from the rooftops as the phalanxes march below. Much has been written about their contribution, and I have attempted to synthesize their ideas into a single corpus—namely, that lending against asset values is highly destabilizing and its effects linger for a long time, thereby drawing the economy into a quicksand of stagnation, details of which I include in Appendix 1 at the back of the book.

THE MURDER WEAPON

Putting the question of the *origins* of crises to one side and turning once more to the role of financial markets as a *propagation mechanism* of shocks in the economic system, what do we have? We know that the drive to create complete and efficient markets—that is, markets that exist to help us to put into effect our plans for the future while disallowing arbitrage—has been an essential, practical consequence of the dominant paradigm. Without a fierce adherence to the tenets of the NEE, we never would have had the explosive growth of financial innovation; the removal of barriers that were seen as arbitrary and encouraging of arbitrage (such as the Glass-Steagall Act in the United States, Article 65 in Japan, or the restrictive practices in the United Kingdom before the 1986 Big Bang); and the replacing of supervision with improved incentives and information as the cornerstones of market functioning.

Yet the economic crisis we are in the midst of seems to have the financial markets' fingerprints all over it. The argument of people like Minsky is certainly a direct challenge to the dominant paradigm. But the response to Minsky's challenge is: show us that the crisis occurred when the markets were complete and efficient and only then will we admit failure. If markets were incomplete or arbitrage existed, then the theory is still valid. Critics of the NEE are being asked to show proof of the absence of imperfection. This is analogous to the falsifying of an ontological statement when the set of possibilities is unlimited.

The proposition is: Crises do not occur when financial markets are complete and efficient. Therefore, since a crisis has occurred, markets must have been incomplete and/or inefficient. To show that this proposition is wrong, one must show that a crisis occurred with full market completeness and efficiency. And if we cannot produce the proof, we must strive for even greater completeness and even greater efficiency. The 2007 Jackson Hole symposium essentially concluded that the convulsion that had then just begun was entirely due to, first of all, incomplete information about who owned what and, second, misalignment of incentives.

Let's see where this argument takes us in the real world. Of course, we know there was arbitrage. Banks invested in structured credit products that they had originated and structured themselves and then placed these products into off–balance sheet vehicles (special investment vehicles, or SIVs, and conduits) that came with their own (temporary, as we found out) source of funding, from the asset-backed commercial paper market. This move merited a lower capital cost than if those assets had been left on the balance sheet. By forcing the banks to have one set of capital adequacy ratios if the assets were on the balance sheet and another set if they were held in off–balance sheet trading vehicles by their investment banking subsidiaries (in line with the so-called Basel Accord requirements), we are told we created perverse incentives for banks to stuff assets into SIVs.

Adherents of the NEE argue that the elimination of Glass-Steagall restrictions in the United States should have been accompanied by removing the Basel-determined capital ratios altogether. Thus each bank would be left to determine its own capital adequacy levels, periodically and lightly examined by the Fed, or other relevant supervisor, which would allow these assets to remain on the balance sheets. This is the key point in their argument: once the structured product assets were on the balance sheets, the newfound transparency of the assets would have made investors sit up and take notice of their risks, and banks' shareholders (represented by the boards of directors) would have acted to check the reckless behavior of bank managers.

The reader can see where this argument is going: according to the dominant school of thought, the answer to our problems was not that there was insufficient regulation but that there was insufficient deregulation.

Yet, there is no evidence that the SIVs were invisible to shareholders. They were reported fully and were there for all to see. Management and shareholders chose not to worry about them until it was too late because there was a *risk blindness* that had overcome markets due to the overoptimism caused by the success of monetary policy. The belief in the market's tendency to produce spontaneous and rational order at a level that is not

apparent to any of us individually but yet is believed to be guiding the system had become overpowering. And that belief led to
our downfall. There were powerful intellectual and ideological
forces that lay beneath this recent crisis, and the crisis that we
find ourselves in—notwithstanding all the signs of recovery—
was the result of an epic intellectual failure.

CHAPTER 2

When Causality
Becomes a Casualty

D ismantling a theoretical edifice as massive and well fortified as the New Equilibrium Economics is a difficult enough exercise without coming up against the skepticism of policymakers who, under pressure from the public, want quick answers to the question: what really went wrong? It is little surprise that American politicians will turn their attention, as they always do during difficult times, to that thing called the Rest-of-the-World, best represented these days in a single word, "China," though one should think of it more accurately as all the economies that generate large current surpluses and recycle those surpluses back into U.S. government securities.

By flooding our markets with its tidal wave of savings, policymakers seem to be saying, China (used here as a synecdoche for all the current account surplus economies of the world) is the reason for our troubles. This excess capital pushed down our interest rates to unwarranted levels and lured our homeowners into the arms of debt. Yet foreign investment in U.S. capital markets was, until recently, viewed as a powerful force promoting globalization and benefiting all parties involved. So what sort of role has China played in the recent crisis: benign or harmful?

The answer is neither. The United States' need for mania-driven capital forced savings out of these countries. It wasn't excess savings pushed from China into the U. S. economy that was the problem at all; it was excess investment triggered by a financial innovation run amuck. I'll explain further in this chapter.

THE POLICYMAKERS' DILEMMA

With characteristic immodesty, Dean Acheson, President Truman's secretary of state, called his biography *Present at the Creation*. From his vantage point—the top diplomat for a victorious power that had emerged from a destructive war in far better condition than any of its allies, and in a position to shape the world according to its interests—he could be smug about it. In contrast, those who have presided over the near demise of the financial system should not be feeling as confident that we have the blueprint for a new financial order. They must first understand what caused the financial system to so nearly collapse.

There is no dearth of potential culprits. At some base populist level, the near collapse is about greed (bankers, subprime mortgage borrowers, politicians); elsewhere, it is claims of incoherence (the regulatory system) and conflicts of interest (credit rating agencies). But in the policy world the search is on for deeper causes. Here, global imbalances appear to be the prime culprit.

GLOBAL IMBALANCES: THE "AMERICA THE INNOCENT VICTIM" VIEW

An early hint of the influence of global imbalances on the crash—in fact, well before there were any signs of a crisis in the credit markets—came from Ben Bernanke, who at the time was a governor on the Federal Reserve Board. In a speech in

Richmond, Virginia, in 2005, Bernanke offered an "unconventional explanation of the high and rising U.S. current account deficit":

> That explanation holds that one of the factors driving recent developments in the U.S. current account has been the very substantial shift in the current accounts of developing and emerging-market nations, a shift that has transformed these countries from net borrowers on international capital markets to large net lenders. This shift by developing nations, together with the high saving propensities of Germany, Japan, and some other major industrial nations, has resulted in a global saving glut. This increased supply of saving boosted U.S. equity values during the period of the stock market boom and helped to increase U.S. home values during the more recent period, as a consequence lowering U.S. national saving and contributing to the nation's rising current account deficit.[1]

Although the subject of his two talks (an earlier one was in St. Louis, Missouri) was the U.S. economy's current account imbalance, he must have been responding, in part, to a challenge from then chairman of the Federal Reserve Board, Alan Greenspan, who in February of the same year had wondered out loud why long-term interest rates had not—as theory dictated—responded in an upward manner to the raising of short-term rates from the summer of the year before. While addressing the U.S. Congress, the Fed chairman called this lack of response a "conundrum." Yet this raises the question: what do worries about the United States' balance of payments and the failure of long-term rates to respond when the central bank is raising short-term interest rates have to do with the stability of the economy?

But, first, some background. This was not the first time that analysts had noticed a large-scale recycling of U.S. current account deficits from the developing world back into the United States. Bernanke's was only the first of many interpretations of this phenomenon that considered the specific implications for the United States. A more benign and generalized version had been offered by analysts at Deutsche Bank a year earlier. In this version, they cleverly termed Bretton Woods II an "unofficial" center-periphery arrangement not unlike the earlier, official Bretton Woods agreement in the immediate post–World War II years, where devastated countries would follow export-led growth strategies and the United States became a willing buyer of their goods, thereby causing U.S. trade deficits to be recycled back into the United States in the form of foreign purchases of U.S. assets.[2]

GLOBAL IMBALANCES: THE BENIGN VIEW

But let us view global imbalances more closely. The benign view explains net capital outflows from countries running large trade and current account surpluses by saying that what matters is not the quantity but the quality of the capital. Under this system, developing countries export more capital than they receive, but the financial capital they import is of a higher quality. What they receive is principally foreign direct investment (FDI), which often brings technology and skills transfer. Since emerging economies want FDI, they must put up collateral with the FDI-producing country.

So, in effect, China recycles the United States' current account deficit back into the United States by buying U.S. Treasuries as collateral, thereby maintaining its undervalued exchange rate by creating an artificial, that is, not strictly necessary, demand for dollars. The Treasuries are held by the U.S. government—actually custodized at the U.S. Federal Reserve Bank in New York—so that the U.S. government could seize these assets if the FDI were nationalized or otherwise expropriated in China.

Of course, it doesn't quite work that way in the real world, but the idea of collateral is to offer some kind of assurance to those private parties who directly invest capital—embodied by technology and management skills—in China so that in the absence of strong property rights, the risk of appropriation is mitigated. There is nothing novel about the idea so far; something similar was used to restructure the debt of less developed countries in the early 1990s. In that instance, a debtor like Brazil put up collateral with the U.S. government in exchange for debt reduction from the Western private sector bank creditors. The clear understanding was that if it failed to service its debt, it would lose that collateral. But the similarities end there.

The Deutsche Bank authors emphasised that in Bretton Woods II, the collateral is accumulated through net export surpluses, instead of Treasuries. This gives the word "collateral" a deeper meaning—it is the goods and services already sold to the goods-consuming country (that is, the United States). They have been purchased with borrowed funds, in the form of U.S. Treasury debt. When the U.S. government seizes the foreign government's U.S. Treasury holdings, the U.S. economy keeps all the goods and services already delivered in earlier periods. In a roundabout way, China's current account surplus is its collateral.

The Bretton Woods II framework solves the puzzle of the high price—in terms of financial instability—that developing countries frequently pay for international borrowing by eliminating the external vulnerability implicit in being a net international borrower. China actually becomes a net creditor through its exporter surpluses, but it received a more desirable form of capital. That is to say, the amount of collateral China was putting up through the purchase of Treasuries—ipso facto its current account surplus—was many times greater than the FDI it was receiving from all the Western countries combined let alone from the United States.

At the time it was presented, this was an intriguing proposition that signified a persistent low-interest-rate world and a concomitant current account deficit for the U.S. dollar reserve currency. It also suggested that worries about the "endgame," that is, disorderly flights out of the U.S. dollar resulting from global imbalances, were overdone. In other words, the Deutsche Bank authors thought this was a highly stable arrangement and worthy of being imitated by other emerging economies. The "revised" Bretton Woods was expected to continue for a long time, with no side effects for the U.S. economy. This was the first of the benign explanations about global imbalances.

The Deutsche Bank thesis paved the way for a consensus to emerge around the relatively simpler idea that the demand for dollar assets by foreigners was related to their need to acquire stable stores of value that could be disposed of easily if and when required—provided they were not seized by the U.S. authorities first for some breakdown in the compact of international trade. Note, once more, the idea has its roots in the theoretical notion of complete financial markets that we discussed at some length in Chapter 1, that the availability of investment products that are needed to allow economic agents in these countries plan for the future is insufficient domestically, so the agents must invest internationally.

A related thesis is that emerging countries cannot create enough trustworthy saving vehicles to keep up with the pace of economic growth because their financial markets are repressed, or "incomplete" in the terminology of the Hirshleifer-Radner theories we learned about in the earlier chapter. Households need to plan for future contingencies, and so they seek out assets that meet their precise requirements (payoffs for expected states of nature). But the supply of financial assets locally is so skimpy they must go in search of them abroad. Unavoidably, investors show up on American shores since the size and depth of U.S. capital markets make the United States the natural and most attractive destination.

OR ENOUGH BLAME TO GO AROUND

A third view of account imbalances is that these large foreign reserves held by countries like China were insurance for its domestic banking system. This view should be attributed to work done by two United States–based economists, Ricardo Caballero of MIT and Pierre-Olivier Gourinchas of the University of California, Berkeley. These economists argue that "excess" international reserves are a safeguard against a sudden flight by not just foreign investors but also by domestic savers in the larger emerging economies—again, China is the one that is always cited—and that the need to build a fortress of foreign exchange is especially great in these cases because these economies have a high ratio of broad money to GDP.

What this means is the money supply relative to output is great and that creates a potential danger. If a severe crisis (for whatever reason) should strike, there is a risk that there will be a rush by bank depositors to pull their money out and seek safety in a foreign currency like the U.S. dollar. The monetary authorities in these countries are therefore wise to accumulate foreign exchange reserves to absorb the outflow of domestic funds. Of course, the central banks could also impose all sorts of controls to prevent the outflows, but that is widely held to be more harmful to confidence of both foreign investors and domestic savers.

What all of these explanations, with the exception of the Bretton Woods II hypothesis, have in common is that they take Bernanke's premise of a savings glut as their starting point and then furnish some elaborate structural reason for why this is so. But the *Economist* magazine, in one of its special briefings, would have none of it:

> An unsatisfying implication of the literature on the saving glut is that it paints America as a tragic victim of forces beyond its control. The emerging markets' need for insurance, in its

many guises, drives them to export capital to America (and to similar places, such as Britain). America, by implication, has no choice but to make room for it.

In fact, Asian savings may have provided the rope; but America hanged itself. The macroeconomic forces that drove the capital flows . . . were met by microeconomic failure. . .

Faced with strong external demand for AAA-rated assets, the financial system got creative. Marginal home loans were packaged into supposedly safe securities. That supply of credit lifted house prices and spurred a boom in residential construction, which filled the gap in demand left by sluggish business investment.

As these loans turned bad and losses mounted, it became clear that banks had set aside too little capital to protect themselves against unexpected losses. That left the banks crippled and the economy on its knees. The villains in this story are the banks for making silly loans and regulators for not insisting on more precautions.[3]

But even the *Economist*'s explanation makes it sound as if the phenomenon works like the two ends of a double-handed saw, that a surfeit of savings was pushing into U.S. financial markets and ingenious American banks were pulling them in happily. Putting blame to one side, which end of the saw moves first? The thinking expressed in the quote above leaves us with no doubt that the push comes before the pull.

REVERSING CAUSALITY

Yet let us stop for a moment and turn cause and effect on its head. We should never underestimate the power of ideas, especially when deployed in the service of profits. A little excavation is in order.

Consider this passage from the recently published book *Credit Derivative Strategies*. That this book came out in 2007 is no reason to believe that this argument was not being used by structured credit analysts "pitching" to money managers with a fixed income mandate from large international investors a few years earlier. (I should know because years ago when collateralized debt obligations, or CDOs, that used emerging-market debt securities were in vogue, I was at presentations where "rationales" similar to the one below, were being offered by my colleagues from Citigroup's Global Markets to their clients):

> In this example we first constructed the frontier for the different combinations of sovereign (rated AAA and AA) and corporate bonds (rated A and A-). Then we analyzed the impact of adding a sampled structured credit.
>
> We generated the paths for all the instruments in the current portfolio and the entire collateral pool of a considered CDO tranche according to a simulation methodology described previously. We calculate losses on each path the following way: if the loss came from the original portfolio, it is included as a full loss after recovery; if the loss came from the collateral pool it is recognized only if the previous losses on the same path have exhausted the subordination and the lower bound on the tranche received. *Once the tranche is eaten through (the upper bound of the losses has been exceeded) there are no more losses on that path from the CDO addition.* [Emphasis added]
>
> Then we obtain the distributions of the internal rate of return (IRR) calculated on each path. The risk is measured as a difference between the expected value and the 99.97% worst case outcome of IRR. We construct the efficient frontier for the original portfolio by selecting the weights between government and corporate holdings to optimize the distribution of IRR (ignoring the losses that came from the CDO tranche).

Then we look at the joint losses and construct the frontier for the portfolios in which up to 10% of assets can be replaced with a CDO tranche of a reasonable rating (comparable with the corporate ratings in the original portfolio) with a collateral pool that optimally diversifies current holdings.

When we replace 10% of the portfolio with government holdings with a structured credit instrument (while keeping duration the same) it increases the overall portfolio risk expressed as 99.97% IRR at risk. At the same time, for a 100% corporate holdings portfolio, it is possible to reduce the overall risk by adding a CDO tranche from an uncorrelated collateral pool. *Added to a mixed portfolio (60% government, 40% corporate bonds) this tranche would produce a higher return for the same level of risk, thus shifting upwards the entire frontier. Adding a CDO tranche permits asset managers to achieve improved portfolio efficiency.* [Emphasis added][4]

What is this lead-footed passage telling us? It is giving us a very practical application of modern portfolio theory. It demonstrates to us that not only are there huge benefits to be obtained from holding a diversified portfolio of bonds—because of low correlation of default risk—but there are additional benefits to be had by structuring this pool of bonds into tranches (or levels), with the ones at the bottom most exposed to the early incidence of default losses and the ones above exposed to default risk only after the lower levels have been eaten through (indicated by the first set of italics above).

What makes this the financial engineering equivalent of a freebie—that is, arbitrage, that most desirable of objectives—is that it increases the return for the same level of risk, where risk is calculated from computer simulations of different combinations of default. (The simulations used in the estimation of risk are often Monte Carlo simulations, where because of the uncertainty of the inputs, there is greater than usual dependence on random sampling.)

The important point is that the engineering of returns in this way claims to push the efficient frontier of return versus risk outward; that is, it claims to increase the return for each unit of risk assumed by the portfolio (second italics above). The results of this financial innovation were so compelling that in the corporate debt market, the CDOs widened the yields between the AAA tranches and the AAA bonds that were used within them by creating a demand for those very bonds. And this created a new arbitrage opportunity and in turn increased the appetite for CDOs still further. This was the famous "search for yield" that tripped unthinkingly out of the mouths of so many investment experts just a few years back.

And this might even help explain the Greenspan conundrum that long-term U.S. Treasury yields failed to rise even after the Federal Reserve had signaled that it had embarked on a round of rate hikes. The explanation is that the issuance of structured credit needed to be hedged by banks—which had structured and arranged the issuance of CDOs—with the purchase of long-term Treasury bonds. And why would they do that? Because subprime mortgages (like the epidemic of junk bond issuances two decades before, when we experienced a similarly flat Treasury yield curve phenomenon in the face of Fed tightening) were never seen by the banks who issued these structures as possessing the low default risk that the models came up with. Banks knew these mostly adjustable-rate obligations were risky and would be reset to much higher rates, making payments difficult to service. The central bank would then be forced to halt its tightening cycle, and long-term Treasuries would rally.

We know now that the simulated losses from default—at least the CDOs structured from subprime mortgages—turned out to have been horribly wrong, and the lower tranches got eaten through, as if exposed to acid. And, alas, the third-party credit rating agencies were using the same models as the structuring bank, so the ratings given out were too optimistic. The arbitrage was built on a bed of sand.

But while it lasted, the effect of this "discovery" was electrifying. It did two things, both of which were pivotal in producing the economic crisis we find ourselves in today. First, it created a surge of demand for the asset class that can broadly be called structured credit; second, it created the need for liabilities (or, debt) that could be placed inside the structures and then "tranched." The financial system sat squarely in the center of this arrangement, *not marrying two needs*—as general opinion would have it—*but helping to create them*.

This is how it worked: the discovery of ratings arbitrage— that higher yields could be obtained from these structures than from existing similarly rated nonstructured assets—soon led to another discovery, namely, that there were not enough assets to satisfy the demand for these structures. The growth of subprime and low-documentation mortgages in the United States as well as high-yield leveraged loans in both the United States and Europe was thus a natural response to the deficiency of debt needed for CDOs and other credit structures. More debt was needed as "fodder" for these structures, and sure enough we got a debt boom.

We see this clearly in the U.S. data: combined household and nonfinancial corporate debt increased by almost 50 percent of GDP between the end of 1997 and 2007, double the rise in the debt-to-GDP ratio during the 1980s leveraging cycle, with the steepest increase coming in the 2003 to 2007 years. Public sector indebtedness from 2003 to 2007 fell in contrast to the increasing debt burdens accumulated by the government from 1997 to 2007.

Residential mortgages made, by far, the greatest contribution to the surge, accounting for two-thirds of the ascent between 1997 and 2007. But nonhousing debt also climbed steadily during this time, with noncorporate business borrowing—mostly leveraged borrowing by private equity—also showing considerable strength.

All of this means that we experienced something like a financial-innovation-multiplier-of-credit; which is a way of saying that the traditional credit multiplier—the turnover from deposits in the banking system into loans, some of which come back as deposits, which then become additional loans, and so on and so forth—was now being complemented by something very new, where the demand for structured credit was driving the demand for subprime and other residential mortgage loans as well as certain low-quality corporate loans.

DEMAND CREATES ITS OWN SUPPLY

Let's try to put this in the familiar language of accounting. There are balance sheet and income statement effects that are at work here. The demand for assets to be securitized for the benefit of creating efficient portfolios for investors created its own supply of liabilities, the largest part of which was put on household balance sheets. But since these borrowings had to be put to use, that is, consumed or invested, it meant that the U.S. household sector, and in turn the U.S. economy, had to spend more than it saved, which is of course how it has ended up with a large current account deficit. This is the income statement effect. But the more interesting (and certainly more intellectually provocative) thought is that these extra savings that the United States needed could come only from the rest of the world. Ergo, savings were extracted from overseas savers. The savings weren't being pushed into the United States at all; they were being pulled into the United States.

In this case financial innovation claimed to have found a way to generate higher returns for the same amount of risk—that is, it claimed to have found a way to push back the Markowitzian efficient frontier using a certain kind of household debt as its building blocks. This in turn triggered greater spending on residential investment, so creating a trade account deficit in the U.S. economy, which was then met by higher goods exports from, say, China, who then recycled that export income back to the United States. The argument that the Chinese authorities should not have accumulated foreign reserves—so as to keep their currency stable against the dollar—but should have allowed it to appreciate, is dubious. China "manages" foreign exchange transactions on both the current (that is, trade) and capital (that is, investment) accounts. Had it had an unregulated foreign exchange market as exists in many developed markets, who is to say that those export receipts would not have stayed offshore and made no dent in the exchange rate at all?

As Figure 2.1 shows, the demand for assets created its own supply of household liabilities (subprime mortgages); and the demand for U.S. residential investment thus created its own supply of overseas savings.

So now we are back to where we started—the global imbalances question. Far from being forced to accommodate the flood of global savings that *pushed* its way, frustrating the objectives of U.S. monetary policy, the U.S. economy—and the U.S. financial system in particular—had created the conditions by which savings were *pulled* out of the rest of the world.

In summary then, financial innovation lay close to the heart of the global imbalances problem, both in the simpler and more traditional sense of allowing lending to take place using asset values as collateral, as well in the more recent and

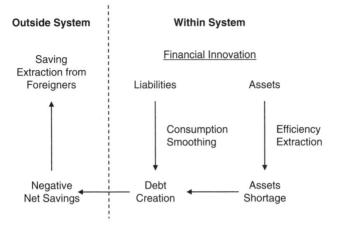

Reversing causality: 1. Demand for assets creates its own supply of liabilities.
2. Demand for investments creates its own supply of savings.

FIGURE **2.1** **Financialization and External Balances**

sophisticated way of wringing efficiencies out of existing financial instruments by structuring them and creating ratings arbitrage opportunities out of them, setting off a frenzied search for more of the same.

MICROFOUNDATIONS OR MACROCAUSALITY

I have presented this demand-pull phenomenon in a deliberately stylized way, and I now need to show how the paucity of savings in the United States translated into a glut of savings in other parts of the world. For this I need to introduce and explore the notion of macrocausality, but since this book is for a general readership, I shall restrict my comments to providing an intuitive understanding of it. I will ask the reader to bear with me as we tackle some of these concepts.

I have previously expressed deep reservations about microfoundations on grounds of both verisimilitude and methodology, but they can be summed briefly as follows: By reducing the workings of an economy to the decisions made by a "representative" individual, we are forced into seeking explanations that depend on nonobservable variables. This destroys the theory's predictive and explanatory power and, in turn, makes the theory unfalsifiable.

I proposed earlier that we reverse causality to see how the demand for debt assets within investment portfolios would cause an increase in the supply of liabilities on household and corporate balance sheets. In the same way, I now propose that we turn the core ideas of microfoundations on their head and envisage a world where certain outcomes are determined at higher levels of aggregation—where the units of analysis are *collections* of individuals fused by some common economic bond—and these outcomes filter down to us as signals enabling each of us to *seemingly* optimize our own choices.

We can call such a collective an economy if it has an endowment of labor and physical capital (our familiar factors of production) and (something less familiar) a currency that is freely convertible into other currencies. We treat currency as an endowment because we introduce it with a qualifier: not all currencies are equal. Finally, all economies trade among themselves.

When it comes to currency, the size of the economy matters. Big economies that are closer to the final demand in the global trade linkage (or, to preempt a notion that I will be introducing in the next section, big economies are "further up in the pipeline") have big, or more precisely, influential, currencies. This is not the same as having strong or weak currencies because that would depend on other factors, as will become clearer presently. Rather, it means that swings in this currency will produce collateral effects on other economies. The exchange value of currencies is determined by flows of financial (distinct from physical) capital. Just so that we do not confuse the two kinds of capital at this stage of our discussion, we will refer to financial capital as "flows."

It will be apparent to most readers that our stylized economy is, in the broad terms in which it has been described here, not too unlike the economies we live and work in. The United States has a big economy endowed with large quantities of both factors of production; demand from within its borders for global products is consumed rather than re-exported, so it sits high on the global trade chain. It has an influential currency that whether weak or strong produces side effects on other economies. And the value of this currency against others is determined by net flows.

El Salvador, on the other hand, has a small economy. It is endowed with small quantities of factors of production, it sits low on the global trade chain, and it has a minor currency. Whether weak or strong, its currency has few if any effects on other economies. China lies somewhere between the United States and El Salvador; it was closer to the latter in the early 1980s, and it is now much closer to the United States for all the obvious reasons.

Influential currencies have an automatically large payoff in terms of net inflows. But flows are also determined by returns on investment. Besides, policy in these economies is not impotent. Much can be done to augment or mitigate these flows by making the destination of these flows, that is, the investment opportunities, within these large economies attractive or not so. Nevertheless, large economies have a lower bound constraint on payoffs, and small economies have an upper bound constraint. What this essentially means is that there are limits on how little and how much in terms of net flows a large and small economy, respectively, will receive. This might help explain why the U.S. economy continues to attract foreign inflows even as it remains in the grip of a severe downturn.

On the other hand, the returns on investment depend on the *relative price* between outputs and inputs. When the prices of commodities are falling but the prices of goods that use commodities as inputs is stable, it helps the relative price of the manufactured goods and hurts the relative price of the commodities. When the prices of intermediate goods are falling and the prices of finished goods are stable, we see the same effect on the relative prices of each. So we would expect flows to move with relative prices. And if economies tend to be dominated by certain kinds of sectors, then we would expect them to receive large inflows when those sectors boom and their currencies to appreciate. This concept is fundamental to my idea of a Super-Cycle, and in the next few chapters the reader will see vividly this phenomenon at work.

But if the attractiveness of any investment is in part determined by the unattractiveness of the investment in the inputs (the so-called relative price argument), and if we can predict when these relative prices will move, then we can say confidently that flows move autonomously and in predictable ways. This concept is critical to the SuperCycle.

But when an economy's policymakers adopt policies that encourage inflows at a time when the country is already receiving large net inflows for relative price reasons, then the conditions are being readied not just for waves to be lapping upon the shore but for a tidal wave of financial capital to come crashing through the sea walls and flood our markets. But in the years leading to the recent crisis, the United States' policymakers, who could at least have stood like Canute, rebuking the advancing waters, even if all in vain, simply left it to the financial innovators who, not knowing any better, invoked the spirits of the deep.

This now prepares us for introducing the notion of a Super-Cycle. Shifts in relative prices mobilize the SuperCycle, and it gathers speed and force when policies perversely encourage its devastating effects. Macrocausality is an overlay on the workings of this global phenomenon helping to explain why some economies—by their sheer size and the influence of their domestic policies—end up magnifying the power of the SuperCycle.

The Wheel of Misfortune

I do not know which makes a man more conservative—to know nothing but the present or nothing but the past.

—John Maynard Keynes,
The End of Laissez Faire (1926)

CHAPTER 3

SuperCycles and Their Laws of Motion

E conomists have long seen the global economy as the aggregation of many national economies, whose business cycles impinge on each other. The idea of a SuperCycle requires us to banish that picture from our head completely and think of the global economy as one very large structure where sectors rather than countries experience violent fluctuations that send shockwaves rippling through the rest of the structure. What are these sectors? They are points on the production pipeline that runs from commodities at one end to finished goods and services at the other. The SuperCycle is the force that pushes disinflation through this pipeline creating booms and busts as it traverses the pipeline's entire length. Such a global framework is indispensable if we are to get a more sophisticated assessment of risk and a deeper understanding of what we can do to thwart future shocks, and, at least as important, getting out of the crisis we find ourselves enmeshed in.

BEYOND THE BUSINESS CYCLE

The idea of a business cycle was losing its appeal even before we found ourselves caught in the jaws of a contraction that mashed up all our notions of cyclical excess or shortfall. Consumption and investment plans in the U.S. economy and elsewhere were turning down with a speed that did not appear to be consistent with the signals that various purchasing managers' indexes were sending on labor costs, business inventories, and new orders. Among academic researchers and staff economists, who bring their latest ideas to the yearly summer fest in Jackson Hole, the thought that the economy's output exhibited a traditional business cycle pattern of restricted length and amplitude had long been suspect. So when Professor Robert Hall, a leading light among macroeconomists and the head of the National Bureau of Economic Research's Business Cycle Dating Committee, proposed at the 2005 symposium that the U.S. economy's real output and unemployment exhibited qualities that were "at frequencies below the business cycle but above long-term trends," he was announcing an obituary for a notion that to the lay mind seemed robust.[1]

Yet these changes are mere curlicues on a larger pattern. Professor Hall may argue that the model he presented not only emphasizes the irregularity of productivity growth—the "shocks" that were discussed in the earlier part of this book—but also movements in exogenous spending that appear to be contributing to the volatility of real GDP. But frankly, who cares? These concerns may have seemed admirable at the time of an obsession with the Great Moderation, but when crisis hits and life is wayward again, then surely the time has come to look at life anew.

This section of the book is written around a few interlocking themes. The central idea is that of an economic SuperCycle, in which a world economy characterized by a high degree of integration in production, trade, and capital flows (in other words, a world very like the one we have lived in for the past 25 years or so) will find itself trapped in a spiral of rolling deflations. If left unattended—and this is where we find ourselves today though less from neglect than from a failure to recognize the nature of this phenomenon—we will escape this outcome only through inviting inflation and so embarking on a spiral of rolling inflations instead. The downward spiral is slow and grinding; the upward spiral is fast and dangerous but, as I shall argue later in the book, inevitable.

Heightening the ferocity of the SuperCycle is our commitment to an exchange rate system that has lulled us into a belief that "flexibility" is a virtue. Put another way, a global economy with a single currency and a single monetary policy would have experienced a much milder form of the SuperCycle. I recognize well that such a global arrangement is a tall, if not impossible, order given the geopolitical realities of our times, and in fact it may never exist, but it is an idealized outcome of the theory I lay out. Yet the paradox of flexibility in our present economic order is that our attempts at adjustment at every stage of this long cycle, while appearing to pull us out of each crisis, were only cumulating troubles for a much larger future crisis.

The lessons of the Classical Gold Standard era, approximately 1870 to 1930, are salient in this respect. The world economy, also highly integrated then, experienced a milder and contained version of the SuperCycle precisely because policies did not allow flexibility. Still there was a need for a systemic anchor, and that role was played unerringly by Great Britain for much of the early years of this period. It is a model that we would do well to consider adopting. As Britain retreated from this role following World War I, and no other country stepped up to take its place in a convincing and committed way, the stability of the system fell apart, the panics became worse, and the Great Depression descended upon many parts of the world economy. That was how a relatively mild SuperCycle came to a bloody end with the Great Depression of the 1930s.

The 1930s have recently become a preoccupation with economists and laypeople alike. Yet a fundamental premise of the SuperCycle idea is that the Great Depression, severe though it was, short-circuited the process of the Classical SuperCycle. Had policymakers' responses been different—that is, had they chosen not to liquidate supply but rather to stimulate demand through monetary expansion by abandoning the Gold Standard earlier and forestalled the worst of the bankruptcies and banking crises—it would still have brought us to a point similar to where we are today. The late 1930s would then have been marked by a more highly indebted nongovernment sector—or whatever would have been feasible given the relative lack of depth and breadth of the credit markets of that period—and yet, as the workings of the SuperCycle will make clear, that sector too would have been near collapse under the load of debt. Large-scale fiscal activism would then have become unavoidable, as it has now, even without World War II; and then the world economy would have emerged from it at the other end with inflation and negative real interest rates.

And so in a spirit of pure adventure, intellectual and otherwise, we should consider ourselves fortunate that we are living through the Modern SuperCycle as it plays out to its end with no interruption. Here the government will either rescue sectors buckling under the weight of debt and inflate the debt away dramatically, or it will embrace the Japanese solution that would have the government restructure the debt of the afflicted parties and absorb the losses itself. The second is nothing more than an exercise in transferring debt from one group to another, and if it is not accompanied by actions intended to create rapid price rises that wipe out the huge load of nominal debt, the economy will slowly sink into the slough of deflation. It is also quite possible that we will get a combination of both courses of action, as the American and British policymakers grapple with the yin and the yang of their choices. This will result in an unpalatable kind of stagflation instead. There are tough times ahead, unless policymakers take the correct stabilizing actions as required by the SuperCycle.

But before we get too deep into this discussion, let's fully unpack the idea of the SuperCycle both analytically and historically. Most of us think we have a pretty clear idea of what business cycles are—fluctuations in output and inflation that show persistence in an up or down direction in our data on important components of output or in the variables that lead output itself: employment, real retail sales, real income, and industrial production. We also recognize that business cycles of important economies, like those of the United States, spill over into the rest of the world and affect other economies in ways that are not always predictable but which we know are caused by trade and investment flows across borders.

In other words, a downturn in an economy will crimp demand for all goods, including imports, which will affect the output of the economies that export to it, and their downturn in turn will affect their imports, and so on. Or to take something more topical: banking and credit crises in an important economy like that of the United States produce risk aversion among lenders or simply a flight back to the home currency, which in turn forces a retrenchment in lending across borders and so produces crisis contagion across large swathes of the world economy.

THE PIPELINE AND RELATIVE PRICES

The thesis that I advance here is that these business cycles are superimposed on a deeper-lying phenomenon—the SuperCycle— that captures fluctuations in output and inflation across a unit of analysis that I will call a *pipeline* or a *production chain* or *supply chain*. I will use these terms interchangeably. We should try to understand this concept in its broadest, most general sense and at this stage, not worry about whether it exists within a national economy or across many economies.

A pipeline is the flow of goods from commodities to intermediate goods to finished goods and services. We should think of this flow not just for any one good but for all goods. So we should think of the entire world economy as being nothing more than a long and wide production pipeline transforming raw, crude commodities into goods, which in turn are transformed into other goods, at each stage achieving higher degrees of completeness, that is, at every stage moving closer to being consumed.

These do not have to be goods in the classic sense. We could include services in this framework since many services—not just final consumable items—also are *inputs* into the production of goods or other services that are finally consumed. So software services, consulting jobs, maintenance of infrastructure, and so on are in no way less central to the production of material goods than, say, a component in a piece of machinery. The production pipeline, therefore, at a still higher level of generality, is a flow of inputs into outputs that in turn become inputs in the next stage of the pipeline, and so on.

Given our highly integrated system of trade today, we see this production pipeline extend across national economic borders in a far greater way than ever before. The extent to which the "assembly" of goods and services crosses national borders before finally being consumed is one of the most remarkable features of our era of globalization. This is well known and has been exhaustively studied. We will see later that the existence of so many currencies floating or potentially floating against each other contributes enormously to amplifying the effects of the SuperCycle.

But the amplification of effects is not the same as the effects themselves. Our present interest is in the Laws of Motion of the SuperCycle. **What gets the SuperCycle moving and then keeps it in motion are misalignments in relative prices.** Let us call this the **Second Law of SuperCycle Motion.** (Why not the first law? Yes, well, more on that later.) It would help the reader to remember our simplified and stylized framework: Commodities are inputs into producer goods, which are inputs into consumer goods, which are inputs into labor, which is an input into all of the rest of the pipeline. By bringing labor into the picture, we have introduced an element of circularity into our framework, and this will be made clear as we examine the workings of the SuperCycle.

What this means then is that when the price of an input, say, commodities, falls and the price of the goods that use commodities as an input—producer goods and hence the output in this case—stays the same, we experience a change in relative prices, or as economists like to call it, the terms of trade of one kind of good versus another. That is to say, the price of commodities relative to producer goods has fallen; or, conversely, the price of producer goods relative to commodities has risen. Either way it is a misalignment in relative prices.

Producer goods and their numerous gradations—core, intermediate, and finished—are both and at the same time inputs and outputs in this pipeline, as are consumer goods and labor. These producer goods in the production pipeline should be seen in terms of their relative prices to their nearest input and output neighbors.

So in the mind's eye of the reader, he or she would do well to recap the essential stylized fact we are presenting here: The world economy is at all times a vast production pipeline that flows in one direction, from primary goods to finished goods of every kind, to services and finally to labor. Throughout history, the pipeline has run mostly inside a national economy's borders; and almost as if in parallel, each national pipeline replicates those found in other similar national economies. But in the modern and industrialized era, the pipeline has become more global—lengthening and widening and traversing national boundaries.

Of course, we can think of this as being a *system* of pipelines since even in the most global of times, there will continue to be full pipelines that remain national perhaps because transport and logistical costs are very high, perhaps because it contains an infant industry that has not yet grown to multinational size, or perhaps it is constrained simply to satisfy a locally powerful constituency. Among the advanced economies, Japan is a good place to look to see plenty of domestic pipelines even as the global pipeline runs through the country.

If this idea of a production pipeline—whether national or international—is so central to our framework, how should we be seeing national economies? They should be seen cross-sectionally, that is, as a cluster of pipelines, some complete from end to end, others part of the global pipeline. Put another way, the large economies, like those of the United States, Germany, or Brazil, are clearly a diversified portfolio of sectors and industries positioned at different points on the pipeline.[2] The dominance of services in the U.S., U.K., and Swiss economies means that these economies are front-end heavy. Australia, Canada, South Africa, and Chile, as economies dominated by primary goods production, are rear-end heavy; Japan, India, and Brazil (each for different reasons) have weights more equally distributed. We should keep this in mind so that even as we think in terms of pipelines, there will be constant references to such pipeline effects on the major national economies.

So what are the Laws of Motion of the SuperCycle? We have seen that when a pipeline input price falls, the *relative* price of the item that uses that input improves, all else being unchanged. And all else should remain unchanged as long as the fall in the price of the input was not caused by a fall in the demand for it. The improvement in the relative price, therefore, could be seen as an expansion of the profit margins—not in all cases the same, obviously, since the cost of material inputs could be offset by a rise in nonmaterial, that is, labor inputs (though it has been widely observed and documented that labor cost increases even in inflexible labor markets will lag output increases).

The boost to margins produces the now familiar signs of exuberance: overinvestment, credit booms, expanding employment. Not surprisingly, excess capacity follows, which results in falling (or deflating) prices that afflict the output sectors, correcting the misalignment with the inputs. This process now repeats in the next stage of the production chain. Relative prices once again get misaligned as the declining price of that good now becomes a cheaper input for some other output. Once again, profit margin expansion leads to an abundance of optimism, to overcapacity, deflation, and so on. Like a long snakelike balloon losing air, the pipeline begins to deflate at one end (the bust), which makes the section closest to it on the balloon (the boom) appear to inflate. But then eventually the deflation travels through the entire length of the balloon. Or to change the image slightly, one could think of one of those serpentine superfloats at a Chinese New Year parade, undulating before collapsing into a heap at the end.

THE FED GETS IT WRONG

Seen in this light, the crisis of commodity-exporting Latin America in the 1980s—resulting from the run-up and eventual fall in commodity prices a few years earlier—set the stage for the huge bubble and ramping up of debt in manufacturing-dominated Japan, South Korea, and the "tiger" economies of Southeast Asia in the 1990s. The collapse of goods prices in the manufacturing section of the pipeline was first interpreted by policymakers like Alan Greenspan as the arrival of a shift in the productivity of workers. Rising profit margins in companies in the information technology and telecommunication industries that depended heavily on intermediate goods imported from those regions failed to be attributed to pipeline effects. Instead—and incorrectly, I might add—they were said to be due to better inventory management (itself seen as the result of superior application of information technology) and other ways of extracting efficiencies out of workers.

Ben Bernanke, Greenspan's successor as chairman of the U.S. Federal Reserve Board of Governors, was less convinced that this price collapse was all so benign. At the very least, he saw that the beneficent forces of disinflation, regardless of their causes, risked taking a rather more destructive turn to deflation. In Bernanke's now famous speech as a governor of the Fed, delivered in Richmond, Virginia, on November 21, 2002—much of it devoted to the exploration of the causes of deflation, its economic effects, and the policy instruments that could be arrayed against it—he revived Milton Friedman's idea of a helicopter drop of money on the population below. In another speech at the National Economists Club in Washington, D.C., Bernanke alerted his audience that although outright price declines in the U.S. economy were unlikely, it "would be imprudent to rule out the possibility altogether."[3] A few months later, in July 2003, at the Economics Roundtable held by the University of California at La Jolla, he thought the balance of risks were then moving firmly in the direction of deflation. "Watchfulness is certainly warranted," he now asserted.

These were just his public pronouncements. The detailed minutes from the Federal Open Market Committee's meeting in early 2003 show Bernanke's influence start to take hold in statements like this one: "Members commented that substantial additional disinflation would be unwelcome because of the likely negative effects on economic activity and the functioning of financial institutions and markets, and the increased difficulty of conducting an effective monetary policy, at least potentially in the event the economy was subjected to adverse shocks."[4]

Or consider this a few months later: "For now, however, they believed that arriving at an understanding of the various options that might be employed prepared them to respond more flexibly and effectively to unanticipated developments. While considerable uncertainty surrounded each individual policy option, the members agreed that the effectiveness of these alternative tools, along with the 125 basis points of conventional easing still available, would allow monetary policy to combat economic weakness and forestall any unexpected tendency for a pernicious deflation to develop."[5]

Yet those familiar with the SuperCycle and its attendant price effects should have had ample warning that deflation was in fact moving closer to an economy so dominated by final goods assembly and services as the United States. The wreckage that threatened to wash across American shores was already in sight when Fed Chairman Alan Greenspan was proselytizing the case for a structural upward shift in U.S. labor productivity trends. Yet, no one saw it.

LABOR CLOSES THE LOOP

We cannot get a full measure of the SuperCycle until we come to grips with labor's role in the SuperCycle. In one respect labor is the same as a "good" or a "commodity" in that it is an input. In another respect it is quite separate because it is the source of final demand. How such a deflating pipeline affects labor is a fascinating and crucially important part of the whole story. It is also especially relevant to where we find ourselves in the Super-Cycle these days. Labor—or more broadly, households—is at the "front end" of the pipeline in that all the goods and services that have been produced, processed, and assembled are for its consumption. So given the logic of rolling deflations, labor is the final beneficiary of the deflating pipeline.

Yet labor—and here one must use the term in its narrower sense and not include *rentier* households, that is, those who live off investment or rental income only—is also an input into *every* output at *every* point in the pipeline. Labor as a *consuming* unit unquestionably gains from deflation. But labor as a *producing* unit gains only if it is employed in that part of the pipeline that is experiencing expanding profit margins and from it, expanded investment and greater employment. In other words, labor does well if employed in that section of the pipeline that is experiencing boomlike conditions. Conversely, it suffers if it is employed in those sections that are experiencing overcapacity of output and are facing the imminence of deflation. In sum, labor is better or worse off than other labor depending on where it is situated in the pipeline.

Households—that is, labor as consuming units—at the front end of the pipeline are unique in another way. Gains to them are *self-reinforcing*; by that I mean they gain from the deflation in final prices as does all labor everywhere—ignoring for now currency movements that might aid or hinder these price moves. But here labor is also likely to be engaged in the production of services, which in turn benefits from the falling costs of goods. Services, as mentioned earlier, are largely nontraded items—that is, they are consumed locally where they are offered, whether it be the services of lawyers or those of financial planners, plumbers, doctors, and teachers.

But this essentially nontraded form of production benefits enormously from the deflation in goods in the same way as any other good in the pipeline benefits from deflation of its input; and the labor it employs experiences nominal wage gains and lower costs of goods, boosting real incomes substantially. Labor employed elsewhere in the pipeline does not get the benefit of this "dual" effect.

Well, wouldn't labor further back in the production pipeline also have periods when they benefit from booming employment conditions and so rising nominal income and also a boost in real terms from falling costs of consumption? The answer is no. And so this brings us to the **Third Law of SuperCycle Motion: Relative price misalignments produce positive effects only when they move from back to front.** What this means is that the falling cost of final goods, for example, does little for profit margins for manufacturers of intermediate goods such as disk drives in Malaysia, Mexico, or North Carolina (even if there are any left in the last named). Hence, intermediate labor does not experience anything like the terms-of-trade gain it would if, say, the price of welding equipment or energy fell. And so, while labor engaged in these downstream parts of the pipeline will get a boost in its real income, it will come only from declining prices of what it consumes and not from rising nominal incomes.

Once more, like the deflating superfloat in the Chinese parade, the SuperCycle requires the tail end of the float to collapse to give a (temporary) lift to the front end. But when goods production further ahead in the pipeline begins to weaken and prices in those sectors begin to decline—in effect creating relative price realignment—the resulting effect is one of falling demand, which naturally travels backward through the pipeline and has a repressive effect on the sectors behind. Hence, this idea brings us to the **Corollary to the Third Law of SuperCycle Motion: Relative price *realignments* are in general negative.** In terms of our very own version of the superfloat, it simply means that when the front end starts to collapse, the rear end collapses still further. The collapse of a very large front end—the consumer spending–dominated U.S. and certain European economies and the sizable household balance sheets associated with them—has unsurprisingly sent shock waves coursing backward through the pipeline.

Yet households who are at the front end of the pipeline and are typically employed in service-related economies and who have benefited doubly from disinflation or, even better, deflation in the cost of goods, will do exactly what producers anywhere on the pipeline would do in a fit of exuberance. They will borrow and build up their balance sheets since they expect the good times to roll on. The boom in housing assets was an unavoidable consequence of that unbridled, but, sadly, characteristic, optimism that afflicts all those swept up by the power of the SuperCycle.

So, in summary, what we have is a pipeline of production running from crude raw material to intermediate and finished manufactured goods. Both services and labor are deployed through the pipeline, but there are services consumed for their own sake only by households. Labor derives its noninvestment income from being employed all along the pipeline. Something set the rolling pattern of deflation in motion, creating price misalignments with goods further ahead in the pipeline and realignments with goods behind in the pipeline. And once the process of rolling deflations begins—the downward leg of the SuperCycle—it has an inexorably forward tendency to it.

Our work is not done. We shall next examine some ideas drawn from economic history on what cause or causes set the SuperCycle moving in the first place; and once we have settled on something, we will have our **First Law of SuperCycle Motion**. But, equally, we also need to ask ourselves how it is that the front end of the pipeline got as big and dominant as it did. In other words, how could service-dominated economies like that of the United States, with its large household balance sheets, make the world economy so unstable? This will be treated fully toward the end of the book.

CHAPTER 4

The Classical SuperCycle Part 1, 1873 to 1900

W*e have learned in the previous chapter that the SuperCycle is propelled forward through the pipeline by shifts in relative prices—also called* terms of trade—*between inputs and outputs. These shifts lead to widening and narrowing of profit margins, which when combined with leverage, are the essential ingredients of booms and busts. Economies that are dominated by the affected sectors expand energetically and contract viciously as the SuperCycle passes through them.*

But we haven't yet asked the fundamental question. What gets the SuperCycle going in the first place? In this chapter we introduce the **First Law of SuperCycle Motion: The initial stimulus behind the SuperCycle is the arrival of a monetary standard that promises price stability.** This law is the shot from the starter's gun that gets the SuperCycle in motion. The Classical SuperCycle that can be dated to 1873 was the first of two SuperCycles. It came out of the widespread acceptance of gold bullion as the basis of money and of payments in international trade. The Classical SuperCycle took close to 25 years to really get going before lasting 60 years in all. Despite stumbling badly at the turn of the twentieth century, it makes for an interesting contrast with the turbocharged SuperCycle of contemporary vintage.

THE GESTATION OF THE SUPERCYCLE

Globalization is not a necessary condition for the processes of the SuperCycle to fully unfold. This phenomenon can occur in closed national economies, though such economies would have to be large diversified ones, with sectors that include the full pipeline from commodities to services, for the SuperCycle's complete effects to be demonstrated as powerfully as they are in globalized economies. What is a necessary condition for the SuperCycle is that within the economic system, whether national or global, there is no impediment to the allocation of resources, including the flow of credit. The flow of goods and the flow of capital are as free of central planning and control as possible.

Unquestionably, globalization of goods and capital does make the SuperCycle more powerful. The effects become more intense, both in the booms as well as in the busts. It is clear intuitively why this is so. The far greater disparity of endowments (differences in the cost of labor, the greater abundance of physical resources) in the world economy compared to any national economy means that as long as the movements of savings and credit are not restrained, we would expect production to occur where it is cheapest and selling to occur where prices are highest. This means that when *relative prices adjust* (and that is what drives the SuperCycle forward), the adjustment will be more violent.

Furthermore, the presence of floating exchange rates combined again with the unrestricted mobility of capital makes the SuperCycle still more potent, as we shall see later in this chapter and the next. Authorities in both the Gold Standard and paper (or fiat) money regimes have been aware of all these influences, but I will argue they have too often been lulled into complacency by a stout belief in the self-correcting nature of their monetary arrangements. The central bankers of our paper money era have been especially guilty of this failing.

It is widely held that the Classical Gold Standard era of the late nineteenth and early twentieth centuries greatly resembled our own recent experience with frenetic globalization. That is indeed true in terms of international migration and the flow of capital, but the mid-1870s to the late 1930s—not all of it an uninterrupted stretch of gold-backed money, by the way—did see years of rising trade protectionism, in contrast to our own orchestrated efforts to bring more and more markets into the liberal trading system. Yet despite much more restricted trade, we can discern the clear outlines of a SuperCycle that took shape in the last quarter of the nineteenth century.

We see that although this SuperCycle moved in fits and starts—because the Gold Standard regime that started in Europe in 1873 and was adopted in the United States in 1879 took the greater part of the last 25 years of the nineteenth century to be fully accepted—there were undoubted movements in prices for commodities and secondary goods that produced the relative price misalignments that I have argued lead to booms and their attendant busts. This Classical SuperCycle, existing from 1873 to 1930 in a global economy where the pipeline was much shorter and the financial system more primitive than now, foreshadows the cleaner and much more powerful SuperCycle that we have experienced recently.

By 1900, the Gold Standard begun in 1873 had achieved universal acceptance—a term we would be entitled to use because it did cover all the major economic regions of the world. This acceptance allowed the SuperCycle to hit its stride for the next 30 years, disrupted only briefly by events that were unique to its history, and finally terminating in 1930. The Great Depression, regarded now as the watershed economic event of the first half of the twentieth century, should be seen for what it was: a severe seizure of the United States and a handful of other economies, such as Germany and Scandinavia, who followed a policy of *liquidation* rather than *liquefaction* (a term I borrow from geology, which means turning to liquid, and yet is appropriate when applied to a system that is denied liquidity). That is, faced with excess capacity and an abundance of inventory in goods markets, policymakers in the late 1920s and early 1930s decided that the mismatch between supply and demand was a problem of excess supply rather than an insufficiency of demand that should be solved by reducing supply rather than increasing demand. We have never ceased to remind ourselves that this was the major policy error of that period; and we have so cauterized the memory of it that we are always falling back on demand stimulus measures at the earliest signs of weakness.

THE BIRTH OF THE SUPERCYCLE

The perceptive reader will already have realized that I am moving toward the explanation of my **First Law of SuperCycle Motion.** I have hinted at a connection between the world economy's move to the Gold Standard and the start of the Classical SuperCycle. As such, **the initial stimulus behind the SuperCycle is the arrival of a new monetary standard bringing the promise of price stability with it.** We will understand the general rule better after we see what exactly the Gold Standard achieved, which it did with a bit of help from Great Britain, which played an indispensable role behind the scenes. By allowing its current account surpluses to serve as an automatic support mechanism, Britain enabled this bullion-based system to function very well for an extended period.[1] (See Figure 4.1 for current account balances of countries.) Some have referred to most of this period as the Gold-Sterling Standard.

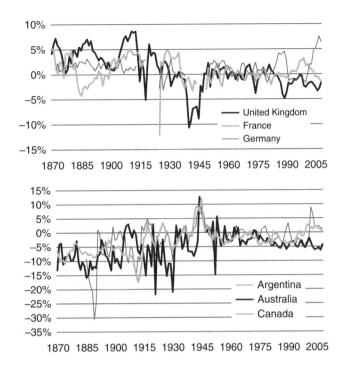

FIGURE 4.1 Current Account Balances as a Percentage of GDP

Source: International Monetary Fund.

But the Gold Standard extended well beyond the period of support it received from sterling. By the early years of the twentieth century, the British government had embarked on a sustained program of spending, a large share of which was military related. As its external surpluses dwindled, it was no longer able to play the role of international lender of last resort. We shall see for ourselves what that did to the stability of the global economic system.

This in turn raises a host of questions about the U.S. dollar's parallel role at various stages and in various arrangements in the twentieth century (for instance, the limited-scope Gold–U.S. Dollar Standard of those few years immediately after World War I, the Bretton Woods arrangements after World War II, and the U.S. Dollar Bloc Standard of recent times). Sterling was eventually no longer able to fulfill its role, and now the U.S. dollar appears to be retreating as well—possibly with equally grave consequences. But more on this later.

This, then, was the dirty little secret of the Gold Standard: it was less different from our own more recent efforts at stabilization than is widely recognized. And in both cases, whether with the Gold Standard of the late nineteenth century or the credibility standard of the late twentieth century (that some have called Enlightened Fiat Standard), there was more of a confidence job at work than many suspected. But that, after all, is the essence of stability: beliefs can become self-fulfilling.

The spread of gold as the backing for paper money everywhere—or almost everywhere—is a fascinating account of the accelerating gains that result as a network expands. We call this phenomenon *network externalities,* and we have seen it in recent years in various industries where the ascendancy of a single standard makes disproportionately large gains possible to its users as the scale of the network increases. For those readers who are interested in the full chronicle of how gold came to rule the global economy, I would refer you to Appendix 2.

But network externalities were not the only appeal of the Gold Standard to its new adherents. The use of gold as a monetary and payments arrangement backed by the enviable reputation of Great Britain as the "real" anchor triggered the move to price stability. Gold was the way to wash off the curse of inflation and the debauchery of paper money as is explained in the rest of this chapter.

GOLD STARTS UP THE ENGINE OF THE CLASSICAL SUPERCYCLE

What did the accepting and implementing of the Gold Standard in the late nineteenth century actually do for the world economic system? Its greatest achievement was that it came to be seen as a stable price system, and that *perception* of stability set off a series of asset booms and busts rippling across the world, producing the Classical SuperCycle. Some of these downturns were quite severe even by the extreme standards of the Great Depression; but that was because financial institutions did not have the safety net of depositor protection under them, and so banks were prone to panics and runs on their deposits.

To understand how the Gold Standard stabilized prices, we must look at the quarter century that preceded gold's introduction as the backing for money. The 25-year time period from 1848 to 1873 was a time of considerable volatility in what was then an industrializing—but still largely agrarian—world. Prices rose sharply after 1853, wages rose with them, and they fluctuated in this higher range until the early 1870s, culminating in a burst of inflation everywhere. Commodities were the main culprit and driving force. Pig iron and cotton prices more than doubled between 1860 and 1873, while copper prices experienced a vertiginous ascent in the five years after 1868. These price increases fed through to wages quickly, therefore causing inflation and creating a situation that displayed all the hallmarks of a wage-price spiral and, in fact, bore an uncanny resemblance to our own recent experience with inflation in the 1970s.[2] Why did this inflation happen at a time when the forces of technological progress were so strong? The swift spread of the industrial revolution throughout Europe and the Western Hemisphere produced its own entrenched belief system—akin to our own faith in the miracle of the supply side—that all these productivity-enhancing factors must have a disinflationary effect on the price level.

The impulse came from the outbreak of wars everywhere. Many economic historians attribute the "Great Inflation" of 1853 to 1873 in no small part to this series of conflicts breaking out across the globe. The Crimean War (1854), the Indian Mutiny (1857), the American Civil War, and the sequence of campaigns known as the Franco-Prussian war that ended in

France's defeat in 1870 were highly disruptive to the supply of goods. Further to the east, China was consumed by the protracted and bloody Taiping rebellion that dragged on until the mid-1860s. Wars tend to produce epidemic-like surges of issuance of inconvertible paper money to finance the higher government expenditure, in turn creating inflation.

Yet another reason for rampant inflation could have been the amount of resources expended on mining precious metals in the 1850s and 1860s. Gold and silver mining in the American West, Latin America, and Australia resulted in a huge diversion of resources—both manpower and physical capital. Yet, even where discoveries were real, they did nothing to add to the supply of goods and services, both of which were experiencing rising demand. Hence, prices of food and clothing and other necessities rose. If so, then there is a certain irony here. Only Great Britain was then using gold to back its monetary system; yet the discovery of large quantities of the metal in the third quarter of the nineteenth century made the gradual and widespread adoption of the gold standard in later years possible.

Nominal wages were also affected by the upward move in prices. Drifting upward over the entire period of 1850 to 1873, nominal wages paced ahead of prices for many years with intervals of sharp advance during phases of intense inflation. For Great Britain, where the statistics were the best organized and most reliable, *real* wages, that is, wages adjusted by prices for consumer items, rose by 35 percent over the 20-odd years after 1853. But, in fact, the short-term pattern was rather more confusing than these synoptic figures might suggest; very often inflation for goods and products would surge ahead, and wage inflation would catch up and overtake it a year or two later. Such volatility is the classic symptom of macroeconomic instability.

Whatever the causes of such price instability during those years, there was little doubt that in the period that followed, the trends reversed abruptly. Following the adoption of the Gold

Standard, the years from 1873 until the end of the century were marked by falling prices. This was the general direction of prices, although the timing and rate of change within various classes of goods, or between wages and goods, varied. The cost-of-living indexes—consumer price inflation adjusted by nominal wage growth—in each of the four major economies show dramatic deflation: the French economy experienced an absolute price decline of about 15 percent between 1873 and 1900, Germany a decline of 13 percent over the same period, the U.K. economy of 24 percent, and the United States a fall of just over 30 percent.

The fall in prices began with commodities, or what would then have been called *primary goods*. The reader will remember that the impetus to the 20 years of inflation that preceded this era of falling prices also came from commodities. A recently constructed industrial commodities nominal price index by the research firm Bank Credit Analyst (BCA) shows that industrial and cash crop commodities experienced an aggregate price decline of 60 percent between 1873 and 1900; pig iron prices dropped by 80 percent, cotton by 70 percent, and copper by 65 percent.[3] Careful data analyses by other economic historians have confirmed that the falls were equally great in lead (65 percent) and in wool and timber (60 percent), but somewhat less severe in zinc (35 percent). The declines were not continuous throughout. The sharpest falls came in the 1870s and again in the 1890s. In rare contrast, the 1880s actually provided some relief to commodity producers. Overall, however, these figures are comparable to the most severe of commodity bear markets we have experienced in our recent history.

CAPITAL FLOWS DURING THE CLASSICAL SUPERCYCLE

But our interest is not in the deflation of commodities prices per se. Our thesis is that relative price misalignments between the prices of commodities and secondary goods put the SuperCycle process into motion. The great chronicler of manias and crashes, Charles P. Kindleberger, illustrates this by examining Britain's prices, excluding the cost of shipping and storage, of exports (mainly manufactured goods) in terms of the prices of imports (mainly commodities) during this period, the last quarter of the nineteenth century.[4] Since this was an era of fixed exchange rates and since Britain had the freest trade system in the world, such an approach becomes a very effective shorthand way of capturing the picture. Kindleberger shows a nearly 20 percent gain over this period in the *relative* price of Britain's exports over its imports. If this is representative of the price "wedge" between primary goods inputs and manufactured goods outputs, then regardless of whether there was widespread deflation in all the major economies or not, the 20 percent gain became a rough proxy for profit margins for manufacturers everywhere. In other words, even if *absolute* prices were falling for all commodities and all intermediate and finished goods, as long as prices for outputs were declining more slowly than those for inputs, that created a gap that corresponded with profits.

And sure enough, we get confirmation of this from another source. This approach looks at the flow of capital from British sources since Britain had by far the world's largest stock of capital, resulting from years of accumulated current account surpluses, which moved freely across the world. Classic works by the British economist A. K. Cairncross and the American economist A. I. Bloomfield both point out the long-term inversely correlated movements between Britain's home and foreign investments.[5] More precisely, the data bears out the inversely correlated movements in economic activity in the United States and Canada (with a sizable and dominant, respectively, commodity sector) and British domestic investments (with a dominant manufacturing sector). In other words, as commodity prices fell, so did British investment into these dominant sectors in the United States and Canada. At the same time, due to relative price misalignments, Britain's goods-exporting economy thrived.

To further prove my point, British domestic investment rose strongly in the 1870s and 1890s—a time of sharply falling commodity prices—thus suggesting that profits were rising, or at the very least expected to rise, in Britain's manufacturing sectors. Foreign investment from Britain did rise in the United States and to a lesser extent in Canada in the 1880s, a decade that provided relief from the relentless deflationary pressures on commodities.

With respect to the 1880s too, the evidence is not without ambiguity. The U.S. economy was becoming increasingly industrialized and increasingly protectionist two decades after the Civil War. Cotton from the U.S. South was now, on pain of export tariffs, being sent straight to the textile mills in the North. The internal market that emerged with the inclusion of the southern states was large enough for the political class in the United States to insist that these infant industries be protected. (It is easy to forget how much of an emerging market the United States then was—and how much of the arguments used by the more nationalist emerging markets today were being used by the United States then.)

While data is not readily available on the precise destination of Britain's capital flows to the United States' manufacturing and noncommodity sectors, other than railroads, it would be reasonable to conclude that the surge in investments in the United States was not due wholly to the revival in commodity prices but some part of it went to the United States' nascent but burgeoning goods manufacturing sectors. This means that the relative price differential in favor of manufacturing did not quite reverse in the 1880s in any significant way.

The critical lesson from this period of the early Gold Standard then is that as gold came to be seen as a sound basis for backing money, and *as the realization took hold that signing on to gold also meant signing on to possible British capital flows as a shock absorber during balance of payments adjustments, the Gold Standard led to an abrupt fall in both inflation and inflation volatility. But more central to my thesis, it opened up a wedge between commodity prices (input prices) and prices of intermediate and finished goods (output prices), which as we discussed earlier is the real engine of the SuperCycle.*

THE EFFECTS OF THE SUPERCYCLE, 1873 TO 1900

The perception that gold would eliminate the severe price instability of the third quarter of the nineteenth century became self-fulfilling. We saw how commodity prices had led the way up during the Great Inflation of the 1850s and 1860s, and we saw how they led the way down in the deflation of the formative years of the Gold Standard era (1873 to1900). We also saw how the price of goods had followed commodities more sluggishly in both directions. So for a goods producer during the inflation period, it was a difficult time since the cost of inputs was rising faster than the price of outputs. Equally, the deflation period that followed was a time of profit since the cost of materials was falling faster than the price obtained for the goods produced.

Credit ineluctably followed where profits were being made. The high inflation years pushed lending into land and commodities but also into the building of railroads—the means to bring the rich agricultural and mineral lands of the U.S. and Canadian West within the grasp of the industrial heartlands in the East. When commodity prices went into steep decline with the increasing appeal of the Gold Standard in the early 1870s, it is no surprise that a banking panic followed due to the large amount of credit that had been extended to the commodity-producing businesses. This Panic of 1873 and 1874 led to the failure of almost a hundred banks in the United States alone.

Now, we've seen how the slowly forming Gold Standard was less of a hindrance to credit expansion than is often mythologized. And in places like the United States, which were still unconvinced about gold, the restraints on credit were minimal. The crash in commodity prices widened margins for those goods using commodities as an input. Inevitably bank lending—after an initial period of reluctance due to the string of bank failures from the 1872 to 1873 panic—picked up once again, this time into industry and land speculation in the industrial Northeast. Again, a string of bank failures followed a few years later, resulting in the Panic of 1884.

And it was in the 1880s, as the spread of gold appeared to falter for a while, that we experienced the fury of the unwinding SuperCycle. Commodity prices in the 1880s again experienced a short, sharp bubble, but this time it was the South American countries, notably Argentina, which felt the brunt of it. British capital that had gone into Canada and the United States in earlier periods now discovered the attractions of Argentina, Chile, and Brazil as well as Australia. Argentina saw a particularly large inflow of capital, especially in the building of a railroad network. Its imports soared even as wheat and other primary export prices climbed. The trade deficit doubled between 1885 and 1889 and the current account deficit, which now included sizable interest payments to British and other creditors, reached 20 percent of the country's GDP.

ARGENTINA ROILS THE WATERS

Even by the standards of Argentina's later indiscretions, the recklessness with which this inconvertible paper money economy was managed in the late nineteenth century was astonishing. Domestic credit and money supply expanded rapidly. The monetary base—the currency in circulation and the banking system's reserves held by the central bank—grew at a yearly rate of 20 percent. Inflation began to climb, and since the Argentine peso was not on the Gold Standard, there was little to stop the government from devaluing its currency against the "hard" currencies, namely, sterling, the German mark, and the U.S. dollar. The devaluation was supposed to increase the value of their export revenues—then priced in sterling—when converted into pesos. But since the country's debts were also in sterling, the gains from one were neutralized by the losses on the other. Argentina eventually defaulted, and we got the famous Barings Crisis of 1890. The effects of this crisis—Britain's refusal to recycle its surpluses to finance other countries' deficits—spread across the world causing the stop-start movement toward gold to pick up again in the 1890s.

As contagion spread from this early emerging-markets crisis to the rest of Latin and North America and even as far away as Australia (another key producer of commodities), and the impetus toward gold was renewed again, commodity prices went into a sharp tailspin for the second time in 20 years. As a result, the Latin American economies were swept into the spiral of inflation and devaluation, each feeding the other, until they all finally moved to gold at the turn of the new century. For them it would be the first of their two "lost" decades. But once again it was a boon to the manufacturing centers of the world economy since their primary inputs had suddenly become cheaper. The SuperCycle that had got off to a strong start in 1873 was now getting a second wind.

EMERGING-MARKET CONTAGION AND POPULIST POLITICS: A NINETEENTH-CENTURY ACCOUNT

A slight detour is in order here. The political consequences of moves far away from the root of all the troubles should not be ignored. The Populist movement in the United States—still an economy with a large commodity sector—was gaining support on the back of these falling commodity prices, which declined still further as Argentina and Chile devalued their currencies and so lowered the sterling and dollar prices of their exports in international markets. The United States, which by this time had been on gold for more than 10 years, found that its commodity exports had become uncompetitive. The problem wasn't just the deteriorating terms of trade for the farmers and miners where the prices of the goods they produced were falling faster than the prices of the goods they consumed. As with all other instances of overoptimism about the future, they had run up large debts too. In a way, each American farmer was facing the same forces as those arrayed against Argentina: deflating prices for products and a large stock of debt. Defaults by the farmers were inevitable, and soon these defaults spread to the railroad companies who depended so heavily on buoyancy in the commodity markets. Almost 570 banks in the United States failed during the panic and the downturn that followed.

That's when the Free Silver movement took off and the United States' ambivalence toward gold returned. As with Argentina, the United States had been running a negative balance on its trade and current account throughout the 1880s, though not on as vast a scale. British creditors had sensed that many Argentine and, quite likely, Australian borrowers would not be able to service their debts, and that now familiar response, an aversion to risk, crept into their dealings. British capital flows could no longer be counted on as a balance wheel to hold up the Gold Standard. The "hard money men"—as John Kenneth Galbraith called the bankers and their supporters in Washington[6]—found that they must compromise on the Gold Standard or contemplate some form of protectionism.

The delicate balance in the U.S. economy between gold, silver, and paper money (the last convertible into either silver or gold at predetermined fixed rates, and the total value of notes plus silver was equal to the value of gold) was disturbed when the supply of silver was increased on congressional authority. This was tantamount to an increase in money supply, and the fixed rate against gold could not hold. Gold had become more expensive than the official rates of exchange. As a result, a run on gold stocks began, ending in the Panic of 1893. Despite the interventions of the hard money men, led by J. P. Morgan, who could cash in on his reputation in Europe to replenish the U.S. Treasury's gold reserves, the double-dip recessions of 1893 and 1896 that followed were harsh. The battle between the Populists and the forces of the Establishment (though they were not called that then) would carry all the way until the elections of 1896, each blaming the other for the mistakes of the past.

CRISIS IN THE GOLD STANDARD

What does this test of the Gold Standard in the U.S. economy have to do with the SuperCycle that was set in motion 20 years earlier? In an era of relentless deflation, political pressure that was organized by the Populist Party and the agrarian wing of the Democratic Party to thwart the workings of the SuperCycle exposed the contradictions of the monetary regime that underpinned the economy. Increasing the supply of silver was what we in our contemporary age would call a "liquidity-expansion measure," no different from the bank rescues that the central banks, notably the Fed, have attempted during our recent crunch. But unlike our own Volcker-Greenspan-Bernanke Credibility Standard, the Gold Standard was defined by a strict rule of conversion of all kinds of money into gold at some fixed price. The Bank of England was routinely able to pull off these types of adjustments because of the subtle workings of its discretionary policy, namely, in its use of the discount rate to expand and contract bank credit.[7] But in a young, fast-growing, rough-hewn, and tumultuous society like that of the United States, the political stresses and strains were hard to manage and populist solutions such as the above were to be expected.

Looking back, the mid-1890s crisis in the Gold Standard was easy to see and explain. A strict rule-based system like the Gold Standard can be unforgiving. The straitjacket of fixed exchange rates for gold would be loosened again and again (a kind of cheating) despite all the expressions of probity and the panics that would ensue.

A cleaner working of the SuperCycle under the Gold Standard, that is to say, with minimal intervention, would have allowed the deflation in commodity prices to feed through positively into goods manufacturing, which it did in all the major economies outside of the Americas. In fact, the success of these economies—Britain, France, and most of all Germany—winched the U.S. economy out of its depressive condition. Exports from the United States grew quickly, and its current account problems soon faded. By 1900 the world economy was growing in a synchronized way again, and the belief that if all the trading countries were on gold they would be spared the troubles they had just come through, seemed to make eminent sense.

CHAPTER 5

The Classical SuperCycle Part 2, 1900 to 1930

The Classical SuperCycle—staggered and protracted—played out over a period of 60 years, beginning in the 1870s and ending at the start of the Great Depression. In the framework of the SuperCycle, wars play an important role because they disrupt the unfolding of the grand economic narrative of the expansion and contraction that follow the relative price misalignments. In some cases wars even terminate this cycle, but while World War I had a disruptive effect on the Classical SuperCycle, the war did not end it. Instead, the Classical SuperCycle played out to its natural end—a significant realignment of prices in the world's most developed economies that resulted in the Great Depression, a needlessly severe downturn resulting from policymakers' ignorance of the damage created by weak aggregate demand.

BREAKDOWN OF ORDER

This book is not an essay on international relations nor is it my place to make broad assertions here; but it is hard to deny an intuitive connection to be made between the commitment of the powers that back an economic system, including the monetary and payments arrangements that support it, and the success of that system. Even with the clear dominance of Britain over other nations in the late nineteenth century, and its still greater willingness to underwrite—through the Gold Standard—the stability of the economic system of international trade and payments with its ability to shift its surpluses among deficit countries, all was not smooth sailing. It is a central thesis of this book that the SuperCycle would repeatedly frustrate efforts at economic stability.

Yet the absence of such a power, or its retreat from a central role, as was the case with Britain after World War I, does not easily derail the SuperCycle once it has begun. The momentum the SuperCycle has acquired keeps it moving. The Great War simply parted the waves, after which the sea was joined again and the SuperCycle picked up where it had left off. The Gold Standard—which had been suspended due to a breakdown in the payments system during the war—was restored after a pause, economies were stabilized, and international trade picked up again.

Expanding the reach of the Gold Standard in the years leading up to 1900 to all the countries on the periphery of the world trading system and the reaffirmation of a commitment to the standard by the United States was to be expected in light of the instability of those years. The panics and downturns in the U.S. economy had been noted by the authorities everywhere, but also noted were the most likely causes of that upheaval—especially the domestic mishandling of the boom in commodity prices in the South American economies. Drawing them into the larger net of the standard seemed an obvious solution to the recurring problem of economic instability that risked spilling over into other countries.

COMPROMISE REPLACES CONVICTION, AND STABILITY BIDES ITS TIME

The renewed commitment by the United States to the Gold Standard should have reinforced deflation tendencies in all commodities and goods. But no sooner had the global membership in the Gold Standard bloc increased, then the system began to be compromised. The United States had weakened the arrangement by allowing its banks to issue notes equal to the value of the government bonds that it had sold in exchange for the gold it had acquired during the Panic of 1893. In John Kenneth Galbraith's words: "The result was a prompt increase in the note circulation of the national banks—in the next eight years it more than doubled. All good financial men praised the step as necessary for the growing commerce of the country—a sound and beneficial action."[1] Additionally, the issuance of currency in the distant lands of Argentina, Chile, Ceylon, and the Philippines could hardly be rigorously monitored. The result was the return of a rate of inflation last seen 40 years before. This time, inflation would continue until World War I and on through to 1920.

Given the realities of national politics, we can sympathize with policymakers' wishes to have a greater amount of monetary discretion in their own hands than could be had under the strict regulations of the Gold Standard. The memories of the deflationary 1890s were raw, and there was an inclination to say "Never again," though it was a sentiment shared more widely in the commodity-producing parts of the world than in the commodity-using regions like Europe. Yet how this could expect to be reconciled with a rule-based system like the Gold Standard is a mystery, and how this could be received without objection in the European economies, where deviations of the monetary base from the gold stock were relatively minor, is a greater puzzle still. The answer to this general sense of complacency is *probably* to be found, as I had stated earlier, in the gradual withdrawal of Britain from the role of impresario of the system and, equally, the failure of anyone else that would be acceptable to all others to fill that vacuum. A feeling of fatalism had come over the participants of the system. Life was ebbing out of the monetary arrangement.

THE SUPERCYCLE STAGGERS FORWARD

Because the Gold Standard was showing weakness, the commodity price deflation of the 1890s was followed in the first decade of the new century by a price spiral upward, feeding into wages but more sluggishly into the prices of manufactured goods. It was now the turn of the industrialized sectors to feel the squeeze of the SuperCycle. This was a difficult time to be a producer of goods, since margins were tightly compressed and profits were sinking. The resulting Panic of 1907—in which there was a run on the banks—was bred by disillusionment of the Wall Street banks with traditional lending to traditional borrowers and by the attractions of extending credit to investors speculating on frothy commodity markets.

The World Bank is the best repository of data on the historical terms of trade between manufacturing and commodities across the world economy for the whole of the twentieth century. A 1988 study by two World Bank economists, Enzo Grilli and Maw Cheng Yang,[2] updated later in 2007 by three European economists, Stephan Pfaffenzeller, Paul Newbold, and Anthony Rayner,[3] is a rich vein of information on commodity prices—and more valuable, their relative price against manufactures and the broad basket of U.S. consumer goods—from 1900 onward (see Figures 5.1 and 5.2). What makes this work so important is that it is free of the traditional notion of terms of trade *for* countries but instead measures them *across* countries for the global economy as a whole. It is in fact a snapshot of the relative price misalignments between the different points in the supply chain, the engine that powers the SuperCycle.

The Grilli-Yang chart shows that the relative price of commodities against manufactured goods had risen by 50 percent from the turn of the century to the start of World War I. No economy with a preponderance of manufacturing did well in this period. The only "developed" economy that showed a shift toward profits between 1900 and 1914 was France, and it was a slight shift at that. Goods producers in Britain, Germany, and the United States all suffered drops in output. Japan, a relatively new entrant into the league of fast-growing and heavily industrializing economies, was particularly hard hit given its dependence on commodity imports.

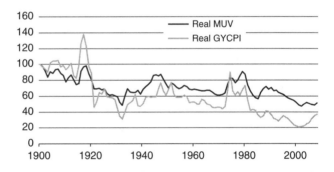

FIGURE **5.1 Commodities and Goods, Deflated by U.S. CPI**
Note: Real MUV and Real GYCPI are goods and commodities prices according to the Grilli-Yang Index deflated by the U.S. Consumer Price Index, respectively.
Source: Stephan Pfaffenzeller, Paul Newbold, and Anthony Rayner, "A Short Note on Updating the Grilli and Yang Commodity Price Index," World Bank Economic Review, *vol. 21, no. 1, 2007. Pfaffenzeller, Newbold, and Rayner adapted this chart from a chart originally developed and published by Enzo Grilli and Maw Cheng Yang, "Primary Commodity Prices, Manufactured Goods Prices, and the Terms of Trade of Developing Countries,"* World Bank Economic Review, *vol. 2, no. 1. 1988.*

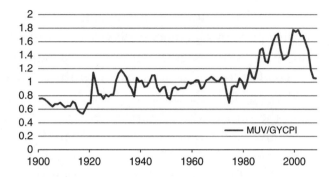

FIGURE 5.2 Secondary Goods Deflated by Commodities

Note: MUV/GYCPI is the price of goods deflated by the price of
commodities according to the Grilli-Yang Index.

*Source: Stephan Pfaffenzeller, Paul Newbold, and Anthony Rayner,
"A Short Note on Updating the Grilli and Yang Commodity Price Index,"*
World Bank Economic Review, *vol. 21, no. 1, 2007. Pfaffenzeller,
Newbold, and Rayner adapted this chart from a chart originally developed
and published by Enzo Grilli and Maw Cheng Yang, "Primary
Commodity Prices, Manufactured Goods Prices, and the Terms of Trade of
Developing Countries,"* World Bank Economic Review, *vol. 2, no. 1. 1988.*

So we come to the eve of World War I with the SuperCycle
staggering forward, the result of a breakdown in Britain's moti-
vation and ability to act as a balancing wheel. By 1910, Britain's surpluses had dwindled, and it was fast losing its creditor
status (see Figure 4.1). The contrast with 1880 when Britain led
the charge to a new international economic order was striking.
Further signs of weakness were evident in the major changes
that had occurred in the British trade and payments pattern.
Negative balances with the United States had risen, and Canada, the Straits Settlements of Southeast Asia, and South Africa
had all become net creditors of the United Kingdom. Additionally, South America was no longer a major debtor. Britain's current account, in other words, had started to deteriorate not just
on the trade balance but also on the invisibles account—which,

as described earlier, was the means by which Britain was able to recycle its surpluses and thus support the Gold Standard by mitigating its harshest features.

In fact, if it had not been for the captive market for its goods in India, Britain's descent would have been still more shocking. Had it not been for the major surplus Britain ran with India, its total current account deficit would have been 60 percent higher. India, in turn, ran a large surplus with the rest of the world. By this time, tariff protection was being raised high everywhere, but Indian exports faced low barriers for a variety of different reasons, the most important of which was that its share of exports was not so large in any of the countries as to attract attention. In a roundabout way, Britain was able to stem the even more rapid weakening of its balance of payments.

Commodity prices were reflecting all this uncertainty. The Gold Standard was under pressure; its future was uncertain. The credibility that Great Britain lent to the standard was disappearing. This leads us to the **Corollary to the First Law of SuperCycle Motion: The restraining force on a SuperCycle is the weakening of the monetary standard.** In other words, when the Gold Standard weakened, inflation resumed, and the deflationary forces that flow through the pipeline—powering the SuperCycle—were absent.

The events of World War I disrupted, but did not end, the Classical SuperCycle. With the destruction of the old political orders that ensued, and the lack of confidence that Britain showed in carrying out its former role as the linchpin of the global trading system, the United States began to rise tentatively to the challenge. By 1918, the original Gold Standard backed by British capital was a thing of the past, and the U.S. leadership showed a willingness to foster and support a mini–Gold Standard among its allies. Appendix 2 provides more details.

THE SUPERCYCLE SURVIVES THE DEPREDATION OF WAR

With the events of and the economic fallout of World War I as background, what was the SuperCycle doing? We will remember that the powerful upward surge in commodity prices began in the early years of the century when a concerted attempt was made to extend the Gold Standard to all trading nations, in the core as well as on the periphery. When it became apparent that it would be a Gold Standard in little more than name, and when it became even more obvious that Britain was slowly abandoning its role as the bulwark of the monetary arrangement, there was little to stop the vertiginous rise of commodity prices.

As we'll see presently, after World War I, with the return of currency and price stability to some of the former key participants in the old arrangement, the wheels of the SuperCycle start to turn again. For instance, nonfuel commodity prices, according to the Grilli and Yang work, fell by more than half immediately following the end of World War I with the introduction of the new monetary arrangement around the U.S. dollar. This took prices well below the levels at which they had existed before the ascent began 20 years earlier. (A simple arithmetic calculation: A 50 percent increase in prices in 1900, followed by a 50 percent fall, would bring prices down to 25 percent below the starting point.) And while commodities prices rallied briefly again at various points in the early 1920s, they never managed to climb above their levels at the start of the century.

But our interest is in relative prices and not absolute ones. How did prices of manufacturing goods compare to those of commodities? Since commodities were, in the 1920s, in the grip of a strong deflationary trend as a result of the new U.S. dollar–led monetary standard, the absence of deflation in manufacturing goods moved relative prices (or terms of trade) strongly in their favor. This was, in fact, the start of the great boom in profits, the buildup of capacity in the durable-goods industries of advanced economies, and the first sowing of the seeds of the Great Crash of 1929.[4]

To understand how the U.S. dollar–led monetary standard came to be, we must look at attempts to restore the Gold Standard following World War I. These efforts were high on the agenda of the major Western powers even though other attempts at international cooperation, such as the League of Nations, were being threatened with strangulation. The U.S.–led loans that were so pivotal to stabilizing some of its wartime allies now became the basis on which other, mainly European, countries could join and so lay the groundwork for a stable arrangement. This effect began with international conferences in Brussels in 1920 and Genoa in 1922. After the Genoa meeting, large international loans were extended to Austria and Hungary to assist them in stabilizing their currencies and so check the inflation that was coming in through high import prices. Similar arrangements were made for a number of the newly formed Central and Eastern European nations that had come out of the disintegration of the Austro-Hungarian Empire. But the key development was the stabilization of Germany in 1923 and 1924, which was accompanied by the drawing up of the Dawes Plan for the settlement of German war debt.

The Dawes Plan was the outcome of a reconsideration of the German reparations problem that had been made worse by the debasement of the German currency after the war. The Treaty of Versailles (1919) had established the principle that Germany should indemnify the Allies for their war losses, and the treaty created a reparations commission to assess the amounts. It soon became clear that the German government would effectively capitulate to domestic political pressure; it would not be able to accommodate these large payments out of its regular budget without squeezing additional taxes first out of the rest of the economy. This it was not able to do. When the treasury bills it issued to finance the deficit through borrowing started to be rejected, it was left with no choice but to ask its own central bank to finance the deficit. This expansion of the money supply led to accelerating and eventually uncontrollable inflation.

This is a state of affairs that we have witnessed many times since. Although Argentina, Brazil, and Peru in the 1980s were not paying war reparations, their governments' response to the demand of foreign bank creditors—and the governments of those creditors—was to seek to extract payments first from domestic taxes (on the advice of the IMF's Washington Consensus agenda), then by borrowing in the local debt markets, and then finally by resorting to the printing presses, which in turn led to the aforementioned rapid inflation.

And very much like the Baker and Brady plans of the 1980s—named after the two U.S. Treasury secretaries in that decade who tried to arrange some mix of debt-forgiveness for the sovereign debtors with a corresponding and firm commitment to reform—the principle behind the Dawes Plan was designed to give a debtor nation some breathing room, though the structure was obviously different from the later plans. Rather than pay off its obligation over a fixed time frame, the Dawes Plan decided that the amount that Germany would pay each year was fixed—or rather increasing in a predetermined way each year for the next five years—and the time schedule was left open. That annual payment was manageable to the German government and something that could be accommodated easily within its budget. The German government took advantage of this reduction of uncertainty to issue a new currency (the reichsmark) in 1924 and move immediately to gold at the prewar exchange rate of 23.8 cents per gram.

Stabilization was now very much a fact. The nostalgia for the Gold Standard of old still exercised a fierce hold on people's imagination even though the fact that the United States was highly tentative about the leadership role it had assumed during and immediately after the war. Eventually, the move toward a restoration of something that resembled the earlier order was solidified in this U.S.–led standard—now called the Gold Exchange Standard—which had a concert of national currencies play the part that the pound sterling had played in the arrangement of the previous century. Appendix 2 explains the standard, with all its fragilities, in detail. The SuperCycle would have one last furious round before it brought much of the world economy down with it.

THE DEATH WISH

So the weaknesses of the international system, even if recognized, were not regarded as fatal. With falling commodity prices (now 10 percent below even the depressed levels of 1919 to 1920) and the terms of trade swinging toward goods, manufacturing of goods was now more profitable than ever.[5] We were now back to the Second Law of SuperCycle Motion. There was rapid growth in iron and steel production as well as engineering and auto manufacturing during these years. Shipbuilding was running at a high level, with diesel engine ships increasing as a share of total output from 14 percent in 1923 to 43 percent in 1929. The production of heavy chemicals grew by a third. Textile production expanded heavily in Japan and India. The output of artificial silk rose by 133 percent between 1925 and 1929.

But as one would expect in the workings of the SuperCycle, the profit margins in goods production that came from low input prices fed exuberance, which, in turn, led to overinvestment and to a buildup of surplus capacity. By the late 1920s there was substantial evidence that the boom had passed its peak. Inventory was accumulating. Commodity control schemes—a form of cartelization by primary producers—were now beginning to spread. In fact, in the major commodity-producing regions of the world—Canada, the western United States, Australia, and most parts of South America—the peak of activity had already been reached a year earlier.

Much has been written by many others about the boom in the U.S. stock market that had become so ferocious in 1928 and early 1929 and the Federal Reserve's impotence with respect to the inflows that were feeding the frenzy. Much has also been written about its incompetence in not seeing that its efforts to sterilize the gold inflows during the frenzy were not reversed during the panic. Much again has been written about the flaws in the Gold Exchange Standard, in which we have just seen that balance of payments deficits could be settled in a convertible currency. And France, perversely and in a preview of its actions in bringing down the Bretton Woods system 40 years later, demanded conversion into gold of all its foreign currency holdings, thus bringing the crisis to a head. And, of course, we all know about the fragility of domestic banking systems where no deposit insurance existed.

My intention in this part of the book is not to go over those reasons. It is to demonstrate the workings of the Super-Cycle: the restoration of monetary stability through the new Gold Exchange Standard; the collapse in commodity prices; the appearance at once of relative price misalignments between input (commodities) and output (manufactured goods); the boom that followed in goods production leading to excess investment, credit, and capacity; and then finally the bust as the authorities in the economies that remained on the Standard chose liquidation over liquidity.

And so, the Classical SuperCycle came to a violent end, spreading economic collapse in many parts of the world. With the Great Depression, the world economy spectacularly fell over the brink, and it took years to be pulled back. The eventual rescue came at a price, and that price had to be paid somehow. The enormous fiscal spending in the U.S. economy that was put into place both as a result of the New Deal and World War II effort enormously increased public debt. Debt rose to 110 percent of GDP in 1946 from 48 percent of GDP in 1938. Inflation picked up in the early war years but then took off immediately after 1945. It reached double-digit rates in the 1945 to 1948 years. All the while, the U.S. government kept nominal interest rates low; so as inflation rose on the monetization of debt by the U.S. central bank, real rates went deep into negative territory. Since inflation stayed high, this negative real borrowing rate allowed the government to easily reduce its amount of debt. Since tax revenues were linked to inflation (and therefore rising steadily) and the government's borrowing costs were held artificially low, the U.S. government was soon running "primary" budget surpluses which allowed it to pay down their debt. Federal debt expressed as a share of GDP was back at 45 percent by 1960. Only inflation and negative real rates made this drastic and relatively easy debt reduction possible. We will refer a few times to the United States' experience from this period later in the book when we argue the case for a quick burst of inflation as a way of restructuring our current outstanding debt.

But, of course, I am getting slightly ahead of myself here. We would have to wait for the turbulence of the 1970s—when the government's rising debt load was increasingly held by foreigners and chaos and disorder threatened the international monetary system—before the conditions were right again for the SuperCycle to be roused from its slumber.

The Thoroughly Modern SuperCycle

There are and can be only two ways of searching into and discovering truth. The one flies from the senses and particulars to the most general axioms, and from these principles, the truth of which it takes for settled and immovable, proceeds to judgment and to the discovery of middle axioms. And this way is now in fashion. The other derives axioms from the particulars, rising by a gradual and unbroken ascent, so that it arrives at the most general axioms last of all. This is the true way.

—Sir Francis Bacon,
Novum Organon (1620)

CHAPTER 6

Enlightened Fiat Money and the Modern SuperCycle, 1979 to Present

We have seen how gold had outlived its usefulness by the time the Great Depression was over. Or did it? Old habits die hard. The new dispensation that would emerge—the Bretton Woods arrangement—would hark back to the Classical Gold Standard in many ways. Now, with the United States the dominant world power and the U.S. dollar the unchallenged reserve currency of the world, we would get a hybrid system that owed something to earlier monetary regimes but differed in some important ways. Both trade and, especially, capital flows were much more restricted this time around; and this might account for the longevity and stability of the Bretton Woods system. Yet even it succumbed finally to another set of problems—some might call it the contradictions of crudely Keynesian demand-management policies where injections of stimulus were applied each time output growth faltered even slightly, and the political costs of an incipient inflation were met in many of the industrialized economies, including the U.S. economy, with a readiness to appease organized labor with generous wage increases.

The emergence of stagflation—high inflation coupled with low, indeed, stagnant growth—that followed in the 1970s would finally force the hand of the U.S. monetary authorities, who in 1979 in a series of audacious moves heralded the birth of a new monetary standard—the Enlightened Fiat—and the SuperCycle, temporarily forgotten, was now ready to make its comeback.

NOSTALGIA DIES HARD

The suspensions of national currencies from gold forced by the economic and social disruptions of World War I and the Great Depression shattered the old monetary system, but governments did not give up on a return to the Gold Standard until after the final breakdown of all currency arrangements in the early 1970s. In 1936, the Triparty Agreement between Britain, France, and the United States attempted to work back to the Gold Standard, as conditions permitted, through a combination of currency controls, fixed exchange rates, and a system of transfers of capital to enable the balance of payments of countries to absorb unforeseen shocks. After World War II, the agreement evolved into a more widely accepted system, now called the Bretton Woods arrangement. This arrangement sought a quick return to gold (or rather a U.S. dollar standard with the United States' guaranteeing convertibility of the U.S. dollar to gold on all the countries' official reserves, which tended to be held in dollars), with fixed exchange rates and free trade and exchange. The primary historical point is this: even after the traumas of the Depression, there remained a powerful urge to return to something like the monetary system of 1914.

Many economists and policymakers of the 1930s and 1940s wanted the benefits of the old system, that is, the stability of fixed exchange rates, while mitigating its weaknesses, such as the inflexibility of policy. This proved impossible without severe and eventually unacceptable international controls of capital movements—enforced by crude administrative means—and domestic controls on prices and wages. The combination of inflation and unemployment together with the actual and intellectual collapses of what was widely seen to be "Keynesian" policies compelled governments to concentrate their attention on price stability through monetary policy alone. The United States would take the lead here and give us the sacrament of extreme bloodletting from the Volcker era of 1979 onward.

What was innovative about these moves by the central banks of the United States and other advanced economies was that for the first time in two and a half thousand years there was no recourse, and even no reference, to gold, silver, or any other kind of bullion as a backing for money. Once the *reputation* of the central bank as a force for price stability—for this would become the new standard—was established, conditions would once again be ripe for the return of the SuperCycle in a thoroughly modern guise. Policymakers and economic planners who had only the history and the experience of the Gold Standard to fall back on would have been hard pressed to have guessed that a new monetary standard would transpire from just the actions and, eventually, words of the central bank with no precious metal to back those words and actions.

Yet, the period from the late 1940s to the late 1960s was actually a period of economic tranquility for much of the world economy compared to preceding decades. Relative prices—that is, the prices of commodities against manufactured goods and each of them against wage costs—remained quite stable, as the Grilli and Yang data shows. Movement in relative prices, as stated repeatedly, is the engine of the SuperCycle driving vast capital flows to whichever region and whichever sector a wedge opens up between input and output prices. In that sense, the SuperCycle had gone quiet, and this was in large part because capital mobility was now restrained and so curbed from chasing after high returns—which as we have seen is a condition for the SuperCycle.

So why did the SuperCycle not become extinct after the Great Depression? Why did the tranquil period (after 1950 in particular) not continue till the present day? And how did accelerating inflation make a comeback at all, thus prompting a crushing stabilizing response from the Volcker Fed, which in turn unleashed the forces of the SuperCycle?

To answer these questions, we should step back briefly and have a look at the 40-year stretch from the 1930s to 1970s when the SuperCycle had been banished, a period that we could call the *sans* SuperCycle era. We can learn as much about the SuperCycle from conditions that deter it as those that abet it.

Much of the *sans* SuperCycle era, was characterized by, first, the dismantling of the whole trade and payments system that had tightly bound the world economy together for half a century before the Great Depression and, later, its very *careful* rebuilding. By 1937 the multilateral trade and payments system that had emerged in the late nineteenth century was near collapse. A multitude of exchange controls were in place that restricted the flow of trade and investment across borders. Nor were conditions any more encouraging to domestic investment because unemployment was still high and the government was taking the lead in job creation through rearmament programs in much of the developed world.

In consequence, international flows of goods, capital, and labor were retarded. With the outbreak of World War II, financial and commercial restrictions on trade were intensified, naturally, and trade between countries was further reduced. But even while the war was still in progress, it was accepted that efforts would be needed to ensure the proper functioning of the world economy in the postwar years. As indicated in the opening lines of this chapter, nostalgia for the pre–World War I arrangements remained strong, but unlike *those* postwar years, the people in charge this time were certain it was not going to be a return to the old order at any cost.

A fuller account of the Bretton Woods agreements (also a kind of Gold-U.S. Dollar Standard) that was put in place at the end of World War II and the turmoil that followed its collapse is to be found in Appendix 2.

THE MODERN SUPERCYCLE IS CONCEIVED

In 1972 and 1973, for the first time since the end of World War II, the economies of the United States, Western Europe, and Japan were moving in a roughly synchronized way, and by the end of 1973 all the industrial economies were seeing sharp falls in their growth rates, resulting from a loss of confidence in the viability of the Bretton Woods arrangement, which was worsened by the sharp rise in the price of oil.

But it was the widely fluctuating value of the dollar in the post–Bretton Woods 1970s, and its propensity to depreciate against especially the Deutsche mark, the French and Swiss francs, and the Japanese yen, that was to a large extent responsible for feeding into large oil price rises. Such a connection between a weak dollar and increasing oil costs was to be expected. Oil export receipts to the OPEC and other oil-producing economies in Africa and Latin America were in U.S. dollars, yet most of these countries' nondefense imports came from Europe and Japan, whose currencies were appreciating against the dollar. They could thus maintain parity between their receipts and payables only by adjusting the price of oil. The pernicious effects of the breakdown in Bretton Woods were now being felt everywhere. It was as if the stability of output and inflation of the previous 30 years had just been an illusion, and all the troubles had been stored up for a later detonation.

Oil price increases meanwhile were feeding into consumer prices broadly. While the average increase in consumer prices in the Organization for Economic Cooperation and Development (OECD) group of industrialized economies in 1968 had exceeded 4 percent for the first time in 20 years, and then rose to 5 percent in 1970, the critical year was 1973. In that year inflation for the OECD jumped to about 8 percent, followed by an even sharper increase to 13.4 percent in 1974. The synchronized economic downturn in 1973 cited earlier was thus marked by the joint appearance of increasing—and, briefly accelerating—inflation and rising unemployment.

By the end of 1974 several economies were still faring poorly: Japan, the United States, Britain, and Denmark experienced a fall in GDP, and in 1975, widely labeled the "worst year in three decades," 10 of the countries who were in the OECD recorded declines in output. The OECD's average annual rate of GDP growth in 1973 to 1979 was a miserable 2.4 percent, less than half the annual rate of the 20 years between 1950 and 1970. The average rate of inflation during the same period in the same group of economies had nearly tripled to 10 percent compared with the 1950 to 1970 average of 3.8 percent. The phenomenon of stagflation had arrived in the 1970s, almost a hundred years to the date of the peaking of the Great Inflation of the 1870s, the event that prompted the move to gold and set off the Classical SuperCycle.

And since American-dominated thinking in macroeconomics, as explained in our discussion in the first section of the book, saw stagflation as largely a problem of inflation and little else, the search was on for a solution that would find its inspiration in an economic variable rather than the clunky, metallic object that appealed to humanity's most ancient and embarrassingly primitive instincts.

We have seen that, throughout the history of capitalism, the SuperCycle is born out of measures to achieve price stability and thrives in the absence of restraints on the flow of capital (the First Law of SuperCycle Motion). Equally, it withdraws and hibernates when the propensity to invest is weak and trade and capital flows are curbed. Yet it is the failure of monetary standards—whether classically gold based or a hybrid gold exchange version—to permanently vanquish inflation that brings forth the SuperCycle yet again.

This is the **Paradox of the SuperCycle: Rooted in our cease-less attempts to expunge price instability, we either fail, as the world economy clearly did in the 1970s, or we succeed so well that we usher in an era of deflation when we wish for the return of inflation.** This is the lesson of the Modern SuperCycle.

EARLY WARNING FROM LATIN AMERICA

The Bretton Woods era was unprecedented in that all econo-mies, whether commodity or manufactured goods or services producing, experienced a remarkable degree of stability in terms of output and inflation. The breakdown of the Bretton Woods arrangements in 1972 and 1973 reintroduced divergences in economic performance. The loss of confidence in the U.S. dollar was demonstrated in dramatic fashion in rising energy inflation, as sketched out earlier, but oil was not the only commodity to see a sharp rise in prices. Nonfuel commodity prices rose by just under 50 percent in the four years between 1975 and 1979, also due to the weakening U.S. currency. This was a period not unlike earlier ones such as the 1870s and the years just before World War I when the world economy had shed an old skin but had yet to grow a new one.

Latin America, with its strong tilt to commodities, had an outstanding run from 1950 to 1980. The contrast with the man-ufacturing parts of the world during the miserable 1970s was notable as well. Latin American economies had grown more rapidly than the world averages that were cited earlier. In fact, real growth rates in Latin America were higher in the 1970s than in the 1960s, something not seen in any other part of the world except the oil-producing region of the Middle East. High and rising commodity prices were fueling the belief that, in the major commodity economies of the region (Brazil, Argentina, and the entire Andean region), these conditions would persist. The run-up in commodities had occurred in spite of a downturn in the non-commodity-producing parts of the world. The connection between the breakdown of the old international monetary system—the Bretton Woods arrangement and its attendant restrictions on capital flows—and inflation in commodity prices was not evident to either policymakers or businesspeople in the region, nor for that matter to the international bankers who queued up to extend large foreign currency–denominated term loans to Latin America's public sector companies as well as shorter-term revolving credit facilities to the region's local private sector banks.

This surge of capital inflows in a floating exchange rate world—remember, the Bretton Woods system of fixed or pegged rates was gone—meant that the Latin American currencies were now also appreciating against the major currencies. This made imports cheap, and both consumption and investments soared. The current account was deteriorating in most of the Latin American economies, but since corporate investment was rising, this was seen as a "benign" current account deficit. These economies were thought to be able to self-correct their deficits since much of this investment was occurring in precisely the sectors that were currently booming and were expected to boom in perpetuity, namely, in agriculture as well as the metals, mining, and oil industries. Moreover, this triggered a spate of public works projects that were intended to expand the road, rail, and port network, which would, in turn, help the exports of those items. Local banks, also borrowing cheaply in the offshore interbank markets, then fueled the growth of credit domestically.

The Mexican and Brazilian stock markets soared, though both were fledgling markets then. Even more impressive were bank lending rates for the major sovereign borrowers. By 1979 these governments could borrow at less than 3/8 percent over the London InterBank Offered Rate (LIBOR), tighter spreads than some of the strongest companies in Europe or the United States. In truth, considerable overcapacity was being built up in these areas, and Latin America was becoming acutely vulnerable to the risk of a "sudden stop" in capital inflows. This would happen with the arrival of Paul Volcker as chairman of the U.S. Federal Reserve Board in August 1979. The preconditions for the birth of the modern SuperCycle were now in place.

BLOOD AND SWEAT IN PLACE OF TREASURE (GOLD)

In his article "Monetary Policy," included in the collection of articles in the *American Economic Policy in the 1980s*, published by the University of Chicago Press in 1994, Michael Mussa, then still the Economic Counselor at the IMF, wrote:

> The Federal Reserve had to show that when faced with a painful choice between maintaining a tight monetary policy to fight inflation and easing monetary policy to combat recession, it would choose to fight inflation. In other words, to establish its credibility, the Federal Reserve had to demonstrate its willingness to spill blood, lots of blood, other people's blood.[1]

This was the Volcker "experiment" in tight monetary policy in the world's most important economy, taking a page out of the anti-inflation strategy book of the West German central bank, the Bundesbank. But unlike the Germans, who were ever vigilant about inflation and consistently had their monetary policy settings somewhat tighter than everyone else after the falling apart of the Bretton Woods system, the Volcker Fed was fighting a rearguard action.

Eight years after the end of a bullion-backed exchange system and the powerful tailwind of inflation behind it, the newly appointed chairman of the U.S. central bank needed not just to administer shock therapy to the economy but also to develop a set of *rational* long-term rules for paper money that would instill *faith* in the central bank's ability and willingness to keep inflation down. And it was precisely because the United States was by far the most important and influential economy in the world that so much was riding on Volcker's experiment to create that new something to replace gold: *fiat* money, which was anchored in an institution's reputation and its management of the key overnight interbank borrowing rate.

This new system of confidence-backed currency would eventually mean giving huge importance to the financial markets. The markets would now become partners with the central bank in maintaining order—an understanding between two parties not unlike that between the police and local community leaders in dense immigrant areas where otherwise communication might be a problem and the risk of misunderstandings high.

It was this arrangement of rational rules communicated through the markets to the economy that was the means to create trust in the central bank's stewardship of the economy. This is called Enlightened Fiat money.

But the disorderly breakup of the Bretton Woods standard meant that a fear still lurked that inflation might prove more deep rooted than most knew. As covered in some detail in the earlier sections of the book, the counterrevolution against Keynesian ideas was under way by this time. It was led by the Friedmanite monetarists and the germinating Real Business Cycle school of thought; and their influence in providing the intellectual backing to legislate new labor laws cannot be overestimated. These laws in the U.K. and U.S. economies used the threat of unemployment to break the link between wage and price inflation. Paul Volcker himself has conceded that the

Reagan administration's success in destroying the air traffic controllers' strike in 1981 was a key move in support of the Fed's efforts to win the war against inflation.

Elsewhere, the move toward tight money and flexible labor markets was also making headway. The Bank of England's lack of independence had been scorned by Margaret Thatcher's advisors when she sat in opposition in Parliament, but when the Conservatives were voted into power in the summer of 1979, her government trampled on any resistance from the bank to her demands for raising the cost of money. With the temporary exception of countries like France and Sweden, who chose not to adopt a policy of monetary squeeze, most global central banks pursued the same actions as those of the United States and Britain.

Such aggressive response to inflation from the central banks of the developed world sent a pointed signal to the bond markets. Nor did the monetary authorities let up until the end of the 1980s, when the United States found itself slipping into a recession. Again, the bond markets duly noted this strategy. Longer-term nominal bond yields shot higher, and real, that is, inflation adjusted, yields on the benchmark 10-year government bonds in all of the major OECD markets averaged between 5 and 6 percent for the rest of the decade, up from slightly negative real yields in the previous decade.

And in most places, even more than in the case of the U.S. economy, the revolution in monetary affairs was accompanied by a move to divesting state-owned assets. Various OECD estimates for the organization's member countries show that the nationalized sector's share of GDP dropped by half between 1980 and 1995. The ostensible reason for rapid denationalization was that these enterprises were inefficient, produced sizable losses, and contributed to widening public sector deficits, which in turn crowded out private investment and pushed up real interest rates. A more likely reason was that privatizing companies made it easier to break up trade unions and weaken collective bargaining, and so control unit labor costs. This measure has remained a key variable monitored by central banks ever since.

It was the United States that mattered more than any other, and in the United States it was the severity of the squeeze in money that produced impressive results. The measures here were declared a success—whatever the initial deleterious impact on real growth in the United States, a painful double-dip recession in the period 1980 to 1982—and the consequences were exhilarating to those who had been haunted by the specter of ineradicable inflation. Consumer price inflation adjusted for energy and food prices fell by two-thirds between 1981 and 1983. To many observers, Volcker's sledgehammer approach to inflation appeared to be well worth it. Margaret Thatcher's victory in Britain was equally dramatic, but in that country's case, the Bank of England's subservience to the government has rarely been in doubt.

The triumph of Enlightened Fiat money would not become universally accepted until well into the tenure of Volcker's successor, Alan Greenspan, but among policymakers in the United States and United Kingdom, there was already an air of victory. They had indeed invented—discovery was too lukewarm a thought—a new dispensation. And they were right. A pattern seen only a couple of times before, first during the Gold Standard and then in the formation of the Gold Exchange Standard in the 1920s, was beginning to repeat itself. Commodity prices were in free fall; the SuperCycle was stirring at last.

The fall in nonfuel commodity prices during the first half of the 1980s was in *absolute* terms the largest since the 1920s, which itself was a period—in hindsight—in which people should have known that something big was in the works. And our old friend and predictable harbinger of the SuperCycle, the terms of trade for commodities—that is, the relative price of commodities to that of manufactures—was turning against primary goods producers with a vengeance as great as anything we experienced in the pre-Depression period.

Once again, a quick look at the Grilli-Yang chart of *relative* prices updated by the team of Pfaffenzeller, Newbold, and Rayner (Figures 5.1 and 5.2) proves invaluable. In terms of relative prices, the period from 1980 onward to the middle of the 1990s was the worst in recorded history. In fact, as the standard of Enlightened Fiat money took hold, the decline in commodity prices relative to finished goods over this period was over 40 percent, but the fall relative to the full basket of consumer goods that make up the U.S. consumer price index was an even more shocking 75 percent. We did not come anywhere close to this disparity before or during the Great Depression.

So that 40 percent fall in the price of an input relative to the output—or, conversely, the big terms of trade *gain* that accrued to goods producers since the cost of commodities had fallen— meant that we were setting ourselves up for a manufacturing boom of epic proportions. And the alert reader would have already detected some significance to those dates just cited. The mid-1990s was when the manufacturing goods part of the pipeline that had thrived since the early 1980s was collapsing. But through the eighties and for half the nineties, the manufacturers were unchallenged. This is their story now.

IN MANUFACTURING, IT IS SURVIVAL OF THE CHEAPEST

Japan and emerging Asia were the two manufacturing powerhouses of the world economy before China had properly appeared on the scene. But Mexico and its industries right on the U.S. border and spreading southward was a new member of the club. It had been among the first of less developed debtor economies to restructure its external debt under the Brady Plan, and discussions about joining the United States–Canada Free Trade Agreement were proceeding during the George H. W. Bush administration. It was poised to take advantage of the liberal trading rules its North American neighbors had offered it at a time when Mexico's main export, oil, was experiencing declining prices. The U.S. auto-parts manufacturing sector started to migrate to Mexico in anticipation of the passage of the North American Free Trade Agreement (NAFTA). Building materials industries in Mexico stepped up their investment outlays. The newly privatized banks (Banamex, Bancomer, Banca Serfin—hallowed names in the history of Mexican finance) were borrowing heavily in the euro certificate of deposit (ECD) market. There was no other economy in the world that had jumped its place on the pipeline from commodity producer to manufacturer as smoothly as Mexico. This is not to say that others had not tried. The Inter-American Development Bank's 1990 annual report looking back at the 1980s lamented:

> The relative weakness in commodity markets encouraged the Latin American countries to diversify their exports, whose volume grew twice as rapidly as that of commodity exports. During the first half of the decade, Latin American exports of manufactured goods expanded even more than twice as fast as total world trade in this category.[2]

Why is this important? Because the SuperCycle idea tells us that when commodity prices collapsed in the 1980s, once the Volcker revolution was seen to be a success, the major commodity producers who were now laboring under the burden of huge debts and falling prices for their exports saw an opportunity to switch to the fast-growing manufacturing markets. Slowly but surely, they were helping to build up excess capacity in these booming sectors. **The Essential Truth of the SuperCycle does not vary: Booms in one sector are built on the strength of busts in another sector.**

So how big a boom was it in the manufacturing sectors of the world economy? Take Japan, which until the early 1990s was the manufacturing powerhouse par excellence. The index of industrial production, the best measure of manufacturing output, which takes its base as 100, in 1985 peaked out at 130.3 in July 1991. And improved corporate fundamentals contributed significantly to the explosive increase in equity prices—corporate profits increased by almost 70 percent in Japan during 1985 to 1990, most of it from manufacturing firms. And the banks are never too far behind, whenever a boom can be sniffed out. The increased lending to the property market fueled the boom in the prices of both commercial and residential property. Increased property prices boosted the collateral value of small and medium enterprises, and with bank lending heavily influenced by collateral values, the unwarranted exuberance about the prospects for capital gains in both the equity and property markets became temporarily self-fulfilling. This is a familiar story now.

But Japanese investment spending more broadly grew rapidly in the latter half of the 1980s—the ratio of gross private fixed investment to the GDP, for instance, increased by almost 5 percentage points during this period to reach 25 percent in 1990. The capital-output ratio increased markedly in relation to its upward trend as many low-return and high-risk projects were undertaken. These were all signs of a manufacturing boom in its mature phase. But an investment overhang was developing not just in Japan but in all the manufacturing centers around the world. The 1990s would be a contest for the survival of the cheapest.

Japan's manufacturing dominance was already being challenged by the first wave of emerging-market economies as well. The Asian newly industrialized economies (NIEs) of South Korea, Taiwan, Hong Kong, and Singapore were hard on Japan's heels through the later part of the 1980s, and, as mentioned earlier, Mexico hoped to become a Latin manufacturing tiger as well. They would be joined a few years later by the still more newly emerged Association of Southeast Asian Nations (ASEAN) economies of Thailand, Indonesia, Malaysia, and the Philippines. The field was getting very crowded.

So why did these manufacturing giants not all tumble together? Why did Japan go first in 1991, followed by Mexico in 1994, and then by the NIEs and ASEAN countries in 1997? And lest we forget, the United States and parts of the European area also have sizable manufacturing capacities, especially in higher-technology industries. And the Internet and technology-media-telecommunications (TMT) bubble collapse of 2000 and 2001 could also be viewed as an extension of the same phenomenon. So, if a fundamental tenet of the SuperCycle is that we stop thinking in terms of *national* economies and start thinking about a *global* pipeline of production that begins with commodities and ends with households, then shouldn't those economies that occupy approximately the same spot on the pipeline rise and fall in unison? This is where we also need to discuss the malignant effects of floating exchange rates, as I had promised earlier.

We saw during the Gold Standard in the late 1880s and early 1890s how the problems in a commodity-producing and indebted economy like Argentina boomeranged on other commodity-producing regions of the world, notably the U.S. economy but also Australia, triggering a political backlash. Argentina, which lay outside the Gold Standard then, had devalued its currency and so priced its competitors out of the markets to which it supplied its commodities. While that may have mitigated the problems in Argentina, it created problems elsewhere.

Now move the dates around just a little. Instead of the 1880s and 1890s, think 1980s and 1990s; instead of commodities, think manufactured goods; instead of Argentina and other commodity producers in North America and Oceania, think

Japan and other manufacturers in East Asia and Mexico. When faced with a situation of overcapacity, the normal reaction of a producer is to cut prices and increase market share. That is what would happen if the world had a single currency or exchange rates were fixed.

But Argentina cheated, if you will, by devaluing the peso against the Gold Standard currencies, and Japan would have cheated as well by devaluing the yen against the currencies of other manufacturers in the early 1990s. Here the parallel breaks down just a little. Japan was *not* allowed to cheat.

The bilateral trade deficit between Japan and the United States was the largest in the world, and by 1985 it accounted for more than half of the United States' total trade deficit of 3 percent of the GDP. The pressure on the Japanese yen, even more than on the European currencies, through the late 1980s was relentless. It took the form of the Plaza Accord in 1985, where the United States' main trading partners agreed to U.S. demands to intervene jointly to strengthen their currencies; and it took the form of voluntary export restraints, which particularly applied to Japan. The pressure on Japan and the Japanese yen, in particular, persisted even as the profitability of the Japanese manufacturing sector turned down in 1990 to 1991 and the real estate loan book of the Japanese banks turned toxic. Japan was not allowed to devalue its way out of trouble. It faced a period of stagnation and malaise from which, arguably, it has not recovered yet.

What was bad for Japan seemed initially to be good news for the other manufacturing centers in East Asia and Mexico. But the artificial strength of the Japanese yen would turn out to be a Pyrrhic victory for them. Since Japan found itself priced out of its important export markets because of its appreciating yen, its companies did the most rational thing: Japanese foreign direct investment poured into Mexico, Thailand, Indonesia, and Malaysia. Where auto parts used to be manufactured in Japan and shipped to the Toyota and Nissan assembly plants in the United States and Canada, they were now being made in Mexico, adding to the U.S. car manufacturers' parts factories there. Ditto for electronic components that were once made in Japan's manufacturing hubs; these now shifted to Malaysia. Some economies from the original club of NIEs such as South Korea and Taiwan were, like Japan, poor in natural resources and had meticulously developed manufacturing know-how.[3] They did not particularly want Japanese investments since they viewed themselves as challenging Japanese manufacturing supremacy and had already invested heavily in some of these industries. By late 1994 global manufacturing capacity was in a glut, and profit margins were starting to shrink everywhere.

Robert Brenner, the economist associated with the Center for Social Theory and Comparative History at UCLA and someone who has chronicled the causes of stagnation in the Asian and U.S. manufacturing sectors in the 1990s better than anyone else, had this to say about the Korean economy, which was in fact one of the last of the manufacturing centers to capitulate:

> Between 1992 and 1995, South Korea, the region's leading economy, had enjoyed a spectacular 67 percent increase in its annual nominal exports, and by 1994–95 manufacturing profits had soared to its highest point, . . . but the ensuing turnaround could not have been more abrupt. In 1996, as export prices and export values plunged, the South Korean manufacturing profit rate declined by 75 percent and plummeted deep into negative territory in 1997 and 1998.[4]

And then came the boomerang effect of the crisis on Korea and other manufacturing countries back on to Japan's manufacturing sector (or what was left of it) in 1998, followed by second and third round effects on each other:

> Profitability now fell back sharply, as did capacity utilization and investment growth. With GDP going negative by 2.8 percent in 1998, the Japanese economy having never

really recovered from the deep cyclical downturn of 1991–95, recoiled into its worst recession of the post-war period, delivering still another crippling blow to the already reeling East Asian economies, a blow that boomeranged back on Japan itself. Between 1995 and 2000, the average manufacturing profit rate fell a further 15 percent from its average level between 1990 and 1995 and in 1998, 1999, and 2000 hits its nadir. Not surprisingly, during this half-decade the growth of GDP, capital stock and real wages in Japan, as well as the level of unemployment, were the worst for any comparable period since World War II.[5]

The only solution available would be the Argentine one from a century earlier: cheat and allow your currency to depreciate. But when everyone cheats—and everyone is able to cheat because we live in a system of floating exchange rates—we get a beggar-thy-neighbor world, and no one is better off.

Mexico went first in 1994. Output in the Mexican economy contracted by over 6 percent in 1995, but the depreciated peso boosted exports, and the economy was starting to grow quickly again by mid-1996. But now the Asian manufacturers were starting to slip. As confidence ebbed in these economies, the devaluations in Asia began. The period 1997 to 1998 was marked by an epidemic of currency runs. What made these particularly harmful was that in each case the currencies were "managed" against the U.S. dollar, meaning that their central banks had vowed that they would defend the exchange rate bands within which they floated. "Hot money" capital inflows had picked up as some short-term foreign investors bet that the central banks of these countries would succeed in protecting these bands. The depreciation of these currencies put an end to those promises and dashed the hopes of investors. The capital flowed out in torrents. Foreign investors packed their bags and left. Without flexible exchange rates, these crises would have been subdued. And since there is no such thing as a currency crisis without a financial crisis, the consequences in terms of output and employment destruction were severe. Manufacturing had finally capitulated before the power of the SuperCycle.

THE IMF AS THE SUPERCYCLE HIT MAN

The IMF's role had changed since the dissolution of the Bretton Woods arrangement in the early 1970s. It was a supranational organization looking for a role to play. In the 1980s, in the midst of the debt crisis in Latin America and other commodity producers, it took on the role of facilitator and enforcer of the now infamous Washington Consensus. The Consensus was simply—but without oversimplification—the Volcker-Reagan-Thatcher regimen of tight money and deregulation of markets as applied to the emerging world, especially the kinds of places that had resisted reform: India, Brazil, Argentina, and Turkey, the black sheep of the emerging markets. Later, after the fall of the Iron Curtain, the IMF was given the job of "transitioning" the former socialist economies to the Washington Consensus.

But the wholesale destruction of economies that came in the wake of the boom and collapse in the manufacturing world was something the IMF had not prepared itself for. It was to help the stricken economies faced with huge outflows of capital move as quickly as possible to new, devalued exchange rates. This may seem ironic because the reader will remember that the IMF's job in the Bretton Woods era was to help a member economy from having to adjust its pegged rate by providing it with lines of credit to shore up its balance of payments.

This time around, however, goaded by the executive board of the IMF, which in turn took their orders from the U.S. Treasury's Robert Rubin and Larry Summers—both among the most ardent advocates of the Washington Consensus—and their man in the IMF, Stanley Fisher, the IMF monitored the fiscal situation inside each of the crisis-hit economies. The IMF was determined that fiscal policy would *not* be used by these governments to prime their economies (in contrast, the reader would at once note how easily the United States and the United Kingdom have fallen back on government spending to stimulate their economies after their two most recent downturns). The countries and their impaired manufacturing industries would use cheaper currencies to export their way out of trouble. Exchange rates in this SuperCycle—in contrast to the Classical one—were playing a pivotal role in intensifying the swings in the SuperCycle, and the IMF was unwittingly increasing the volatility of output in the crisis economies.

The rationalization used by the IMF and its supporters in U.S. Treasury was that floating exchange rates helped to bring gains to everyone, the sellers of manufactured goods as well as the buyers. By depreciating your currency, they told these economies, you keep your prices constant in terms of your own currency, but lower prices in terms of the buyers' currency. This would stimulate demand for your goods, and all your surplus production capacity would get absorbed.

The disinflation ("deflation" was still seen as too remote a possibility) that this would impart to the importing economies— the United States and Western European countries accounting for most of the imports—would be welcomed by their central banks. It would take the tightening bias off their monetary policy. And sure enough, the Greenspan Fed suspended its interest rate hikes in 1997 as the Asian economies fell.

The bust in the manufactured goods sectors globally was now feeding the boom further along the pipeline. Between 1995 and 2000 unit import prices for capital goods fell by 35 percent in U.S. dollars and by 25 percent in terms of the European currencies that were part of the Exchange Rate Mechanism— the arrangement that was a preparation for the single currency, where individual European currencies moved in tightly controlled bands against each other. The preponderance of these were components for final assembly in the advanced Western economies, or they were finished capital goods. Both types of goods came overwhelmingly from the crisis economies, including Japan. (China had now appeared on the world stage though its contribution to the global glut of goods would be through its supply of finished consumer goods.)

The destruction of the once mighty U.S. manufacturing sector that had led the world in the production of durable goods continued apace; but that is a long-running tragedy and worthy of another book. It was now the turn of the New Economy sectors, the technology, media, and telecom industries in the United States and Europe, which were the main beneficiaries of falling import prices, that would feel the bittersweet effects of the SuperCycle.

CHAPTER 7

Beyond the Great Depression

T he *SuperCycle had laid waste to large swathes of the commodities and manufacturing sectors of the world economy in the 20 years after the birth of Enlightened Fiat money. Its signature was a currency crisis followed by a severe debt crisis. This is the point where in the earlier Gold Standard—the Classical one—misapplied solutions produced the worst economic catastrophe in recent history. But at least some policymakers had learned the lessons of history well. This time when the SuperCycle reached American shores, the world economy would bend but not break. Policymakers would pass their first test, but there was another waiting in the wings. The risk is that this time we think we have applied the solution well, but could we have misdiagnosed the problem?*

A COGNITIVE BLIND SPOT

To Fed watchers and other market commentators, the U.S. central bank chairman's conversion to the New Economy cause in the late 1990s was initially mystifying. But only initially, since many skeptics, including the hedge fund manager George Soros, were soon converted to that cause as well. Alan Greenspan's doubts arose from the effervescence of the U.S. equity markets in the early years soon after the brutal round of central bank tightening in 1994 and early 1995. The equity markets were reading the future differently from policymakers. Worries about inflation were never far from the minds of members of the Fed's main monetary policymaking body, the Federal Open Market Committee (FOMC), but it was not a worry shared by most investors in U.S. stocks, who were paying more attention to the Panglossian strategy bulletins of Goldman Sachs' equity guru Abbie Joseph Cohen—not to mention her even more zealous band of imitators, most notably Ed Kerschner and Jeffrey Applegate of the now defunct firms of Paine Webber and Lehman Bros.—than to the FOMC's statements and minutes.

The failure of inflation to rise accompanied by an acceleration of business investment in the United States' technology sector gave the FOMC a validating argument, if not the irrefutable evidence, that the U.S. economy was experiencing a highly benign form of disinflation. The sequence went something like this: higher investment rates in higher-technology business investment led to higher labor productivity, and since wages, although rising, did not keep up with productivity, this led to higher profits. Ergo, higher stock prices were justifiable, especially since the higher profits were not seen as one-offs due to a reduction in costs but as evidence that the economy was on a steeper path of technological innovation—that mysterious exogenous "shock" that we learned about in Section I, where households would rearrange their intertemporal preferences, causing sharp moves in the economy and asset prices. The thought that a dramatic fall in capital goods import prices owing to the collapse of the manufacturing sectors overseas was *apparently* pushing up labor productivity (because costs, revenue, and productivity are all computed in actual dollar terms) did not occur to the Fed, or if it did, it was not entertained seriously. It had become a cognitive blind spot for policymakers.

Meanwhile, U.S. business investment was running far ahead of internally generated funds or operating cash flow. Business investment spending had risen from 7.5 percent of the GDP in 1993 to almost 13 percent in 1999, during a seven-year period when real GDP had grown by over 30 percent. It meant that in actual, inflation adjusted dollar terms, business fixed investment more than doubled in those years. What was astonishing, though, was that an increasing share of capital expenditure was coming from the information technology and telecoms sectors. Let us hear again from Robert Brenner, that meticulous surveyor of animal spirits run wild:

> Constituting just 8 percent of GDP, information technology accounted for an amazing—and quite unsustainable—33 percent of the economy's total GDP growth between 1995 and 2000.... Taken together, between 1995 and 2000, productive capacity in computers, communication equipment, and semiconductors grew by a factor of *five*, accounting in the process for more than half of the record-breaking increase of productive capacity in the manufacturing sector as a whole in this quinquennium.[1]

Meanwhile, the corporate financing gap, which is the difference between business capital expenditure and operating cash flow, widened, which meant that dangerous levels of borrowing were filling the deficit. The gap was negative in 1991; that is, companies were cash flow positive even *after* investing. Put another way, nonfinancial corporations had money left over even after investing. This turned in a most dramatic way as the 1990s proceeded. By the end of the decade the gap turned strongly positive, to 4 percent of the GDP by the year 2000. The nonfinancial corporate sector was getting seriously overleveraged (Figure 7.1). It was the technology, media, and telecommunication businesses that were the source of much of the borrowing after 1997.

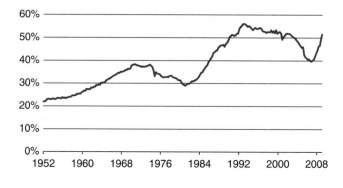

FIGURE 7.1 **U.S. Corporate Leverage, Debt as a
Percentage of GDP**
Source: U.S. Federal Reserve.

So here too we see the familiar SuperCycle pattern repeating itself: a sharp and unexpected fall in the cost of material inputs expands profit margins in certain industries, increasing optimism in those sectors, promoting additional leverage that produces additional capacity. An investment overhang follows. The excesses then start to unwind. Robert Brenner's research is once more authoritative here:

> The core problem was to be found in high-technology lines—microprocessors, computers, and telecommunications itself—which saw their ability to make use of the enormous additions to capacity that they had made during the previous half-decade collapse. Capacity utilization in 1999–2000 in computers, communications equipment, and semiconductors had reached 85.9 percent; by 2001–2002, it had dropped to 59.7 percent. . . . The losses of these firms reported for the twelve months following 1 July 2000 amounted to $148.3 billion. This was slightly more than the $145 billion in profits they had realized during the entire five-year boom of 1995 to 2000. As one economist wryly noted, "What this means is that, with the benefit of hindsight, the later 1990s never happened."[2]

Even using the more generous accounting convention of free cash flow, a measure that allows depreciation and other tax breaks to be added back, the U.S. high-tech industries experienced a drop of just under 50 percent compared to 1997. It was as if the euphoria vanished overnight. A collective delusion that had gripped the markets had now finally been cured.

The U.S. economy may have felt the full lash of the Super-Cycle more keenly, but there were other advanced economies that felt its effects as well. The European economies, including the United Kingdom, had spent much of the 1990s trying to look more American. Creating a single-currency zone was a preoccupation of most of the continental European economies, and the liberalization of domestic financial markets was high on the agenda of policymakers in the run-up to the launch of the euro and the establishment of the European Central Bank (ECB). The more structural aspects of reform—labor market deregulation and changes in competition policy—were at least being discussed openly, inviting speculation that we might at last get the United States of Europe. And while the European countries were not running budget surpluses in the late 1990s as the United States was, at least they had shackled themselves to a commitment (one of the Maastricht criteria that countries would need to satisfy in order to qualify for single-currency membership) that their deficits would be capped at 3 percent of their respective GDPs. The financial markets liked what they were seeing.

The steep fall in commodity prices and the consequent decline in the export prices of manufactured components had benefited Europe as well, though perhaps less so than the United States. This was because the European Exchange Rate Mechanism (ERM) currencies that formed the prototype of the euro in the 1990s had weakened steadily against the dollar since 1995; and for that reason they strengthened less against the currencies of Asia than the dollar during the second half of the decade. This did not prevent the mania surrounding the productivity miracle in the United States from spilling over into Europe.

Investment growth at the high end of the manufacturing chain, industrial machinery, and high-grade telecommunications equipment in particular, grew rapidly between 1998 and 2000 (5.1 percent in 1998; 5.4 percent in 1999; 4.4 percent in 2000). Euro area companies' spending on capital goods finally peaked at just below 13 percent of the GDP in the first year of the new millennium.

The European equity markets reflected the optimism no less than the equity markets in the United States. Valuations of companies in this sector more than doubled during this period. Companies in the region, as in the United States, financed their investment needs with borrowing. And here too they left behind a strong sludge of corporate indebtedness once the tide of optimism retreated. At the peak of the corporate boom in 2000, nonfinancial corporate indebtedness had risen by almost 30 percent compared to 1995. But unlike in the U.S. economy, the borrowing in Europe took the form of bank loans rather than bond issuances, which eventually resulted in banks' tightening lending standards and holding back recovery longer than was the case across the Atlantic.

It was around this time that references to the Great Depression and the Japan malaise became more frequent in both the United States and Europe. The sheerness of the fall in some sectors of the equity markets and the exposure of banks to corporate indebtedness in Europe raised fears that policymakers' resolve was being tested and they would be found failing. It did not hurt that a Princeton professor who had a made a name for himself as a forensic expert in the causes and effects of that great cataclysmic event in the 1930s was now a governor on the board of the most powerful central bank in the world. Governor Bernanke's appeal for monetary activism—which was complemented by tax cuts and, fortuitously enough, increased military expenditure—fell on a receptive audience. The views of his chairman, Alan Greenspan, on the role of money in a modern economy were perhaps less formally articulated, but Greenspan's actions both during the market crash of 1987 and the recession of 1990, as well as during the upsurge of inflation in 1994, suggested that he believed that money mattered and that monetary policy mattered a lot. Something like the Greenspan Approach was now regarded as the guiding principle of U.S. monetary policy. Targeting of policy objectives, such as achieving a core inflation rate of between 1 and 2 percent or cooling down an overheated economy by 1 or 2 percent of growth, would now have to make room for low-probability, high-impact events. What this meant was that if the risk of a negative outcome like deflation, which had ruinous consequences for the economy, had *risen* suddenly from extremely unlikely to very unlikely, the central bank should ease rates to counteract even this low-probability event, regardless of what the economic indicators were saying. A truly negative outcome with a low likelihood of occurring still trumped other more likely outcomes.

The ECB came along as well—lagging as one would expect it to, the result of its newness—with an untested Dutch central banker at its helm, and a general sense of bloody-mindedness among the Germans in the policymaking body who maintained that the Americans were trigger-happy—ready to ease at the first sign of any threat to growth and (although not openly voiced) the profit expectations in the equity market. ("High-beta worriers," was how an economist friend of mine who worked at Germany's Kiel Institute put it to me a few years ago.)

Inflation pressures were ebbing in all the advanced service-driven economies that were users of goods. In fact, in the G-4 economies (United States, United Kingdom, European Union area, and Japan), core consumer goods inflation fell from 1 percent per annum in 1999 to *minus* 1.5 percent in 2004. Bernanke's worries seemed to be well founded. The central bank's prompt and aggressive response, which we will discuss soon, averted the outcome so feared.

So what could have become a mini-Depression turned into a garden-variety recession in the two most advanced economic regions of the world. Seen within the framework of the Super-Cycle, the parallels with the early 1930s were not insignificant. This is how far the SuperCycle had come during the earlier period. It could go no further because much of the world was on a Gold Standard until too late, and the governments in many parts of the world followed what we, looking back now, see as a perverse policy of liquidation. As a result, much of the world slipped into a black hole.

The world economy was then only a *dual-production economy*, dominated by commodities and produced goods. Equally, the financial system then was relatively primitive. Finance existed mainly for trade and business investment. Securitized household finance lay beyond the realm of imagination. All this would change in the next 70 years or so; much of this change would happen at an accelerated pace after the birth of Enlightened Fiat money in the late 1970s. Services would come to dominate some of the most advanced economies, creating a *triple-production economy*. Households in these economies would discover that they had a balance sheet and an income statement similar to that of any corporation, and this would become a source of profit and a source of leverage and risk. The pipeline would thus be extended further. The SuperCycle was moving into territory it had never traveled before, and history would cease to be a useful guide any longer. We will soon be asking ourselves this question: if the SuperCycle is taking us into an unfamiliar landscape, then are we using the *map we have or the map we need*?

ENTER FINANCIALIZATION

If the 1980s was the decade of commodity price deflation, then the 1990s was the decade when the air went out of manufacturing. As the new millennium opened, there were a handful of economies where growth of GDP was dominated by services. The U.S. and U.K. economies were standouts in this regard, not only with their powerful banking and finance industries but also their large media, legal, retailing, and real estate services businesses. Ireland, Spain, Belgium, and the Netherlands have smaller services sectors in the total composition of their output—in fact, in every case smaller than Japan's—but all had seen rapid growth of services. We could also distinguish between economies like those of Germany, Japan, and Australia, on the one hand, whose services industries are rather more dominated by manufacturing-linked services—transportation, logistics, and distribution—and economies like those of the United States and United Kingdom whose finance, accounting, and insurance industries are less dependent on the fate of other sectors in the pipeline.

We could go on splitting hairs of this sort, but the vital point is this: in terms of the schematic of the Modern Super-Cycle, the 20-year process of disinflation that began with commodities and spread to manufacturing was now delivering a strongly positive advantage to all *users* of these items. And in those economies whose output *and* employment were dominated by users of manufactured goods and commodities, it would be their turn in a sweet spot: the cost of their inputs would fall while their income would not. Moreover, at least as important as the dichotomy between services and other sectors is that in these economies, the expansion of household debt as a conscious macroeconomic objective to stimulate the economy had brought the SuperCycle to its final phases.

The identifying marker of this stage of the SuperCycle is that households employed in sectors that have gained from falling input costs (namely, services) and have access to debt that is provided by one of the dominant industries in the services sector (namely, finance) are able to create something like a virtuous circle for themselves. To paraphrase the legendary Polish economist Michael Kalecki: when an economy is dominated by finance, borrowing is a guarantee of solvency.

What this means, again in a highly stylized sense, is that if we imagined an economy where finance employed everyone and everyone had unlimited lines of credit, then through a process of simple circularity (and on the assumption that debtors are not allowed to default but will be given more loans if needed to pay interest), debt becomes a source of income. We could call it the **Munchhausen Principle of Finance** after the story of the Prussian officer who claimed he could pull himself upright by his own bootstraps.

While the U.S. and U.K. economies are by no means so completely dominated by the finance sector that the extreme case of the Munchhausen principle should apply, the expanding reach of finance is certainly related to the idea of Fordism that appeared in the United States, perhaps coincidentally, just before the Great Depression. Henry Ford's avowed plan was to be able to match the wages of his workers to the cost of his cars, so that the success of his company depended on the purchasing power of his employees.

Financialization—the catch-all name given to the dominance of finance in these economies, though the U.S. economy is the paradigmatic example of it—is an extension of Fordism. The financial sector too, by a provision of credit to households, makes its own existence and well-being possible. And as it grows, it becomes an important source of employment by hiring more workers from those households. And also as it grows, it supports the growth of ancillary service sectors that are dependent on it—what economists would call "accelerator" effects, such as accounting and legal services—who in turn hire workers from households who in turn borrow from the financial sector. Meanwhile these households have other needs, say medical and housing, and so spend on these goods and services, and part of the income that goes to those who work in those sectors is spent on financial services. (This is the more familiar "multiplier" effect.) So in a stylized sense, the financial sector has entered into an *entwined relationship with households*, increasingly lending to those who depend on it in other ways. Like Fordism, the dependence is intensely mutual.

And just as Fordism was a brilliant illustration of scientific management, that great contribution of the Progressive Era, so Financialization is an equally stunning practical application of modern economics. Fordism "created" efficiency out of raw nature; Financialization "discovered" efficiency in the laws of nature, making possible an optimal allocation of resources in a market economy. As I argued in the first section of this book, those discoveries are of dubious worth.

But let us now look at how Financialization brought us to this advanced stage of the SuperCycle and how the very tools that we should have used to avert the Great Depression, and which we did use to thwart the dangerous downturn after the technology bubble burst, have created the financial crisis that we have just experienced.

Let me not be coy about my conclusions: the outlook is grim. While history offers many possibilities, it is likely we are entering a period of Japanese-style stagnation in much of the advanced economies of the world, and a thrilling but dangerous bubble in the emerging-markets world, both of which will be followed by a period of very high inflation everywhere.

LIQUIDITY, NOT LIQUIDATION

The memorable words of Hoover's secretary of the Treasury Andrew Mellon, spoken in 1931 (and attributed to Mellon by Hoover, though Mellon denied the attribution) have served as a reminder to policymakers ever since of how to correctly diagnose a problem (a mismatch between aggregate supply and aggregate demand) but badly misapply the solution (reduce supply):

> Liquidate labor, liquidate stocks, liquidate the farmers, liquidate real estate. . . . That will purge the rottenness out of the system. High costs of living and high living will come down. People will work harder, live a more moral life. Values will be adjusted, and enterprising people will pick up the wrecks from less competent people.

As the tech bubble burst, the U.S. Federal Reserve could have followed the purgative approach and allowed the economy to liquidate the excess capacity in segments of the high-end manufacturing sector. The European Central Bank could have done the same, though it would have to be sensitive to the loan portfolios on the books of its banking system, as we explained earlier. Neither (nor for that matter did the Bank of England) took that chance. The U.S. central bank was especially unrestrained in its expressions of worry. The spirit of Milton Friedman (still alive then) presided over the FOMC meetings, and the specter of Andrew Mellon lurked around every corner. Governor Bernanke's speeches that we have cited earlier were both a Eucharistic adoration of the former and a final exorcism of the latter.

In early 2001, the Fed began to ease rates. Rapidly, it lowered rates by 5.5 percentage points over the next 30 months. Between 2003 and 2004, the nominal fed funds rate would fall to 1 percent and stay there. The language emanating from the FOMC minutes, which we touched upon earlier, was written to alert us to the risk of deflation arising in the U.S. economy. It was followed by two years of rate hikes, raising the fed funds rate by 4.25 percentage points. These were the years of Alan Greenspan's bond conundrum and Bernanke's response to an excess of global savings, which we discussed in Chapter 2. The search for yield that ensued promoted the appeal of structured credit products, of which the collateralized debt obligations (CDOs) were the most attractive. Modern portfolio theory provided the requisite justification for the use of these products. This too was discussed in Chapter 2.

Nor was the Fed alone in its easing. The ECB and the Bank of England may not have been the worrywarts that the U.S. central bank was, but they did their share to add to the Great Wall of Liquidity. The ECB's easing cycle pushed down its key policy rate, the refi rate, by 2.75 percentage points in the aftermath of the tech crash. The Bank of England lowered its key rate from 6.0 percent to 3.5 percent as well.

But the spotlight should be on the household balance sheets of the major service economies, of which the United States was by far and away the largest. The SuperCycle had the United States squarely in its sights. Just as the commodity producers had had their years of euphoria and leveraged up indiscriminately only to go bust a few years later, and just as manufacturers had had their binge years of building capacity and accumulating debt only to collapse like so many bowling pins soon after, it was now the turn of the households in the big consumption-driven economies of the West. They were in their sweet spot. Core goods prices had stayed in mild deflation in the G-4 economies (the United States, United Kingdom, Japan, and the European Union area) until the end of 2006. Yet core services prices had experienced mild inflation throughout, as had nominal wage growth in the services sector in the U.S. and U.K. economies in particular. Put this all together and what do we have? That old familiar pattern reemerges: a terms-of-trade gain to pure service sector companies and the workers they employ. Since Financialization fostered the growth of credit to households, the ghost of Munchhausen had appeared.

And what should we expect to happen when credit is plentiful and a household is optimistic about its future—experiencing *real* wage growth in a booming and profitable service sector? It will look to invest in the most leverageable asset available: housing.

The expansion of U.S. household debt through the easing and tightening periods in the first half of this decade was nothing short of breathtaking. The ratio of total household debt to net annual household income (including voluntary retirement savings) in the United States had grown from 35 percent of income in 1952 to 67 percent of income by 1984—a near doubling of the share. Between 1984 and 2000—the period when the entire pipeline of products except the front end collapsed slowly into deflation—the percentage of debt to income rose from 67 percent of income to an astounding 100 percent of income, meaning that the relationship between debt and income had reached parity. With deflationary tendencies now dominant and with households employed in a services sector that now accounted for nearly three-quarters of the GDP, the ratio of debt to income rose even higher still, to 140 percent by mid-2006. In less than six years we had seen a remarkable 40 percent increase in this key ratio.

What occurred in the U.S. economy has occurred with similar force in other economies where household balance sheets expanded under the sway of excessive optimism: Ireland, Spain, and, especially, the United Kingdom. It is in the U.S. and the U.K. economies that the whiplash of the SuperCycle will be felt most keenly.

And so households—and their partners-in-crime, the financial sector businesses—have some serious deleveraging to do (see Figure 7.2). The inexorable logic of the SuperCycle will demand that. The bust in commodities and manufacturing—the two preceding segments of the SuperCycle—produced deflation in the outputs from those sectors. We have certainly seen a very violent deflation in the *assets* held on the U.S. household balance sheets, but I fully expect to see deflation in the price of services that the U.S. produces.

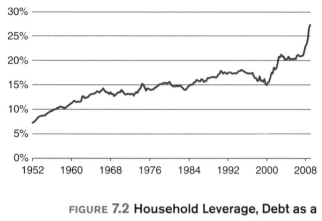

FIGURE **7.2** Household Leverage, Debt as a
Percentage of Net Worth
Source: U.S. Federal Reserve.

The prognosis is not good. Services inflation, unlike goods inflation, has behaved in a remarkably "sticky" way for the last 30 years—as one would expect it to, given the dynamics of the SuperCycle where commodities fall first, followed by manufactures, and only then by services. In the next section we will discuss what will produce deflation in service-dominated economies, such as those of the United States and the United Kingdom, and whether this will be caused by nominal wage deflation. If so, we will have to confront a future very similar to Japan's lost decade. But, depending on the actions of policymakers, we can pursue other options that will allow our service-based economies to avoid Japan's fate. These actions will constitute three scenarios: deflation, inflation, and stagflation. We will also investigate in detail the investment implications of each scenario.

Where Do We Go from Here?

Life can only be understood backwards;
but it must be lived forwards.

—SOREN KIERKEGAARD,
Danish philosopher (1813–1855)

CHAPTER 8

Three Scenarios of Adjustment

The Modern SuperCycle has brought us to a place we have not been before, and thus far our reading of history has served us well. In our current downturn, the leaders of the largest and most affected economies have used fiscal and monetary policies with little concern for restraint. But, as explained earlier, what is new about this crisis is that the household sector in those afflicted economies—mainly the U.S., U.K., and a handful of smaller European economies—are net buyers of goods rather than net producers of goods. This is where the problem resides. Households are the indebted part of the economy, and it is their indebtedness (not that of the corporate sector, which was the primary cause of crises elsewhere in the pipeline) that is the reason for the near-total breakdown of the financial system. Until the household sector in these economies "adjusts" to the rest of the pipeline, we will not have found our solution. This chapter explores ways by which that adjustment could occur.

TIME FOR REALIGNMENT OF RELATIVE PRICES

But, first, why does the centrality of households make this a different type of crisis? In earlier episodes in history when sections of the SuperCycle pipeline collapsed, such as during the Great Depression or the Japanese crash of the 1990s, the household sector was vulnerable because it was employed by the business sector (in large part), and the risk of rising job losses affected total household expenditures. A fall in household spending from a loss of income or due to a rise in precautionary saving thus risked worsening the problem of weak demand. But in the Modern SuperCycle, the feedback mechanism is smaller, tighter, and more vicious. To use a term we came across in Section I, but to use it in a different way here, households are not "exogenous" to the primary demand shock—they are the "endogenous" element. Household borrowing to finance an expanded balance sheet—which itself was the consequence of falling goods prices and greater optimism about the future by being employed in the nonmanufacturing sector—has gummed up the financial system. And the withdrawal of credit available to the broader economy has in turn substantially raised the risk of continued high unemployment. This has added a self-feeding element to the crisis. Now it is businesses, or more precisely nonfinancial businesses, that are the exogenous elements in the initial propagation of the shock, and it is through them as employers that households are experiencing second-round effects. This is the distinctive element of our contemporary crisis.

The efforts of the governments of those economies most affected by this crisis have therefore been focused on averting a meltdown of asset values on household balance sheets and through them onto the financial system's balance sheet. The debate that has taken place—in the United States at least—has been on how best to do this and how much the burden needs to be shared by the two parties involved—that is, the household and financial sectors—and how far the government should go to absorb some of the damage.

Meanwhile, with all the attention being paid to balance sheets and asset prices, the deadly corrosive power of the Super-Cycle has been thwarted. We will remember that balance sheet adjustments can be fierce and excess capacity is often shed painfully through a process of deflation. Left to its own devices, the SuperCycle ultimately forces a realignment of the terms of trade of goods and services all along the pipeline. Everywhere from commodities through the full range of manufactured goods to services we must finally achieve a correction of the misalignment of relative prices. The reader will remember the Laws of SuperCycle Motion from earlier in the book. *Booms arise from a misalignment in relative prices; busts force a realignment in relative prices.*

In other words, the prices of all inputs and outputs through the length of the pipeline *will tend to return to parity.* How should we define price parity? *Price parity* is the set of prices that would hold through the pipeline in the absence of a Super-Cycle; think of it as the prices of inputs and outputs that would hold in such a *steady-state global economy.*

The latest boom came out of disinflationary (and then deflationary) trends in the prices of consumer goods. The terms-of-trade gains accrued to households in large service-driven economies where prices of services and nominal wage gains opened up a wedge or gap. The inflation wedge between services prices and core goods prices had averaged 3 percent per year in the years between 2001 and 2006, the period when this exuberance took hold. Rough calculations using the Pfaffenzeller index for relative price movements—and using the U.S. GDP deflator as a rough proxy for services—would point to a cumulative wedge in favor of services over goods in the U.S. economy since 1980 of about 25 percent.[1] The cumulative wedge between commodities and services was about 70 percent at its worst in the late 1990s, but more than half of that misalignment has been corrected by now (as can be seen in the Pfaffenzeller index until 2006 and making a further adjustment for certain industrial and agricultural commodity prices that continued to rise to the present day; in fact, the misalignment of goods and commodity prices had largely disappeared by 2006). The relative gain to *users* of manufactured goods and commodities through much of the duration of the Modern SuperCycle has therefore been enormous.

So what is the steady-state level of prices? That is a difficult question to answer if we have to do so counterfactually. That is, if we have to look at our recent economic history and try to work out what prices would have been in the absence of liberalized trade and capital flow regimes, in all likelihood we will reach a wrong answer. Instead, we'll look at relative prices in the period when the SuperCycle was dormant—between the Great Depression and the collapse of the Bretton Woods arrangement in 1973.

During this dormancy period, manufactured goods and commodities moved in tandem with each other with an average relative price misalignment of about 20 percent. This means that in order for current price misalignments to be corrected, we need at least a 20 percent move in relative prices—down for services, up for commodities and goods, or a combination of the two. Put another way, it means deep deflation for services, or high inflation for goods and commodities, or high inflation everywhere but relatively higher inflation for goods and commodities, or some combination of all of these things.

We must also remember that exchange rates are flexible and the pipeline from raw materials to services traverses the world economy. How then does the circle get squared? And will government intervention help or hinder this adjustment?

NO PAINLESS SOLUTION

The expansion and contraction at the commodities end of the pipeline in the 1970s and 1980s were not confined to Latin America by any means, but it did affect that region more severely than any other. Like the Emerging Asian episode that arrived in the 1990s, the scale of the crisis was in part determined by the fact that much of the debt was incurred in foreign currencies and held by foreign creditors. On the other hand, the debt profile in the Japanese crisis was different. The debt was yen denominated and almost wholly domestically held.

The recent financial crisis in the United States and United Kingdom—which in fact, was a more global crisis than any of the others, but we'll concentrate on the source points of the crisis—is more complicated than those that preceded it. Although the liabilities are notated in each country's own domestic currencies, the question of who owns the debt has become increasingly unclear, especially in the U.S. case. The U.S. government's intervention in the banking and insurance industries through direct capital infusions, which are then financed through government debt issuances bought by both domestic and foreign buyers, puts the U.S. case somewhere between the Japanese and Latin American cases, though probably closer to the first. In addition, the U.S. government has met only moderate resistance to its attempts to stimulate the economy with additional expenditure and tax rebates. This too makes the United States look more like Japan than Latin America.

Why is this important? Though other variables will have to be considered as well, the U.S. debt profile could give us an important clue about how the SuperCycle could play out, or how the governments that are now managing the crisis response would want it to play out.

The U.S. government is fighting the threat of deflation that the SuperCycle threatens to impose on the afflicted sectors. Deflation in the SuperCycle results from an unwinding of surplus capacity. The damage that this will wreak on household balance sheets and through them on to the financial system balance sheet is the powerful dynamic that the government is attempting to reverse by renewing an appetite for credit. In other words, the government wishes to perpetuate the relative price misalignment between services and nominal wages in the service sector, on the one hand, and all other points in the pipeline, on the other, in order to prevent the deflation of household balance sheets. The giant float at the Chinese New Year's parade is ready to collapse, but the front end is being held up by artificial means. Or to change the metaphor, like Atlas holding up the world, will the combined might of these governments be sufficient to immobilize the SuperCycle?

If household and financial sector balance sheets are prevented from deflating, the authorities believe the forces that are driving the SuperCycle will be stopped in their tracks. (Or rather, since the concept of the SuperCycle is alien to them, policymakers think they can at least partially return to the way things were.) But economic agents in all economies (except the most centrally planned ones) are guided by expectations. This is a variant of the old adage about investors being motivated by fear or greed. Economic agents—whether households or businesses—are motivated by optimism or pessimism about the future. Corporate and household balance sheets expand and contract accordingly, and the pace of expansion or contraction depends greatly on the availability of credit.

The theory I have advanced in this book is that the trigger for an upward break in the investments rate in any sector of the pipeline is the unexpected expansion of profit margins from falling input costs. This is the up leg. The down leg is the unwinding of these excesses. It begins with the realization that far too much capacity has been built up and that there is insufficient demand to absorb the oncoming supply. Then prices begin to fall and the deflation in these goods becomes the way profit margins expand in the next stage of the pipeline. The U.S. federal government intervention, through both fiscal and monetary policy actions, is an attempt to abort the down leg of the SuperCycle. This would not have been tolerated in any of the emerging-markets crises. The Japanese government tried to chart an independent course, but a combination of timidity, lack of conviction, and a rising exchange rate frustrated its efforts. Eventually, deflation prevailed.

The governments' responses to the crisis this time around, no matter how resolute, cannot create the initial trigger that fuels appetite for credit—which is the optimism that results from a surprise widening of profit margins. Attempts to restore the credit markets to their earlier state of functioning will not suffice. Gathering a pile of dry tinder will not produce a bonfire. A spark is needed, and only the SuperCycle with its promise of unanticipated and then seemingly persistent profits provides it. The policy of forbearance that the U.S. government in particular is so intently following is too pat, too convenient, too likely to fail. This is to say that the government hopes its policy of restoring quick functioning to the credit markets and the economy's attendant return to growth will heal the wounds in the household and financial sectors of the economy. Unfortunately, this policy is doomed to lead the economy into stagnation. The price that the SuperCycle exacts must be paid.

It is also quite likely that the present administration in Washington believes America is large enough and resourceful enough to create its own reality (to use a term that came from the mouth of the preceding administration), taking a now inward-looking country in a prosperous new direction, guided by developing self-sufficiency to meet its energy needs and building and sustaining an equitable health-care system.

We are therefore left with three possible outcomes:

- Japanese-like failure of the authorities to foil the down leg, which in turn creates deflation

- Transferring the burden of distressed debt from the household and financial sector to the government, which is then monetized away, resulting in inflation

- Policy confusion, where monetization of public sector debt is alternated with action to preserve the dollar's role as a reserve currency and so keep the U.S. currency strong, resulting in stagflation

THE DEADWEIGHT OF DEFLATION

I have sprinkled the word *deflation* generously through the entire book. My frame of reference, though, has been that stylized construct, the pipeline of goods, running across national boundaries, moving where the most value can be added and ending finally as a product to be consumed. And when I have talked about deflation, I have done so about a certain *type* of good whose price collapses under the weight of excess supply, while those of other goods at other points on the pipeline stay unchanged. Now, even as we keep that concept in mind, we should introduce the more widely accepted meaning of the word, which is that of a general decline in prices in any given economy.

Most economists and economics and investment commentators using that word in its conventional sense draw a distinction between benign and malignant—or harmful—deflation. Benign deflation is what happened in the U.S. economy in the 1870s when the benefits of an expanded railroad network built in earlier decades filtered through to the rest of the economy. Transportation costs fell, large-scale migration of people occurred, new lands were opened up to be exploited, and the rich bounty of those lands was gathered at little cost. The huge volume of goods that came forth created a mismatch of supply and demand which led to falling prices.

More recently, as discussed in an earlier part of the book, Alan Greenspan and the New Economy proponents advanced a theory that breakthroughs in information technology had so increased the power of computing and managing data that this produced a labor-cost saving revolution, which allowed falling final prices to coexist with rising profits. (According to this school of thought, it even resulted in a pickup in investment rates and an expansion of capacity that absorbed the surplus labor, hence creating jobs.)

The reader who has read my earlier sections as carefully as I would have hoped would know that I am completely unsympathetic to these sorts of explanations. I have already offered an alternative explanation for both these episodes. In the first case, that deflation came only in the 1870s and then again in the 1890s when the Gold Standard was slowly being put into effect, thus creating a new monetary standard that in turn spread confidence that the price level would be stabilized. In fact, prices rose in the 1880s when the spread of the Gold Standard faltered.

In the second explanation, that deflation was imported from falling manufactured goods costs, resulting from the collapse of the "factories" of the world between 1990 and 1997—first Japan, then Mexico, and then emerging Asia—which created the appearance that productivity was rising. It does not take a sophisticated economist to know that productivity is measured in nominal terms, that when the cost of the material inputs is falling and the cost of the output is constant, the "other" input, namely, labor, by default is more productive. The phenomenon of benign deflation is at best ephemeral and the rest of the time a mere categorical error.

On the other hand, malignant deflation—the phenomenon of a general fall in prices that produces destructive and self-reinforcing effects in the broader economy such as that of collapsing output and employment—is a fact. Here, my quarrel with mainstream thinking is not what it says about the *causes* of generalized deflation—and I do not disagree at all about its incidence at certain points in history, the unpleasantness of the phenomenon, or the need to do something about it when it does occur. My quarrel is whether it is failing to see a different kind of malignant deflation that regrettably we are walking right into.

The mainstream view on causes of deflation can be summed as follows: malignant deflation can be driven by falls in demand that are greater than expansion in aggregate supply. This typically happens when there are negative money shocks that are nonneutral over a significant period. What this means is that the central bank creates less money than is needed by economic agents to smooth their consumption intertemporally ("negative money shock"), which cannot then be offset by the agents' readjusting their portfolios any other way ("nonneutral"). Once more the alert reader will remember that this was discussed in the early part of the book. Mainstream theorizing cites the recession of 1919 to 1921, the early years of the Great Depression, and Japan's "lost decade" as examples of malignant deflation.

Yet, the mainstream economic theory has little to say about how this deflation impulse propagates itself. Ben Bernanke, the current Fed chairman, has at least tried. He and his coauthors, notably Mark Gertler of New York University and Simon Gilchrist of Boston University, have drawn eclectically on the work of an early-twentieth-century American economist, Irving Fisher, and a more recent heterodox economist, Hyman Minsky—neither of whom until recently occupied a prominent place in the canon of *modern* economic thought—to offer an explanation that runs from deflation to financial distress and back to deflation, and so on.[2]

Fisher argued that it was through something called "debt deflation" that deflation gets entrenched in economies and becomes increasingly hard to root out. He begins with an indebted economy, where businesses in particular had taken on a great deal of debt. Fisher, oddly enough, is silent on the initial cause of deflation, but we could take his silence to mean that he agreed with the dominant thinking at the time—that deflation was due to large-scale imbalances between supply and demand. Once deflation sets in, businesses that have incurred debt at fixed nominal rates are suddenly confronted with rising *real* rates—since inflation is negative. A fixed amount of debt at rising real rates prompts debtors to sell assets and repay loans. When repayment becomes widespread, the banking systems' balance sheet starts to contract—what we call "deleveraging." Fisher connected deleveraging and asset sales with selling inventory, so as the supply of goods from liquidating businesses increases still further, it pushes down prices still more, worsening the real rate of borrowing and giving the deflationary impetus a greater boost.

Minsky, on the other hand, points to a certain kind of lending, the kind that in its extreme and overexuberant form uses asset values as collateral—rather than the traditional kind that carefully estimates streams of future net income to be received by the borrower. The newer sort of lending is the leading culprit in asset bubbles, inflating them and then bursting them. But the real damage—to output, employment, and prices—begins only after the bubbles have collapsed. Since credit is extended on the basis of collateral value, a fall in asset prices produces a retrenchment of credit. Once loans are called in, the Fisherian process of deleveraging begins, leading once again to liquidation of production capacity. Supply comes spilling out, and final prices drop still more. In turn, asset prices fall further, the collateral backing the loans falls again, and the downward spiral takes another leg down. But it is important to remember the differences between Minsky and Fisher; the former argues that it is asset-based lending that finally triggers a withdrawal of credit, whereas the latter believes that the repayment of loans is provoked in the first place by an initial round of deflation and a voluntary repayment of credit. In the Fisherian case, it is private virtue adopted en masse that creates the public sickness of deflation.

Bernanke, Gertler, and Gilchrist draw on the Minskyian idea of collateral-based lending, but they disagree that there was anything inherently wrong with that sort of lending. Their protests should not surprise us. These are after all economists steeped in the finest subtleties of Equilibrium Economics, which we dissected so lovingly in the first section of the book. To them the financial system is the central nervous system of the economy and has the core function of a market economy, which is to allocate resources as efficiently as possible so that consumption and investment plans are optimized. However, the central bank's signals can be misinterpreted and economic agents' plans can overshoot in one direction or another. The unwinding of excess can be painful, and the risk of debtor default compels financial institutions to pull back credit. Credit intermediation jams up, and companies denied credit will now face default where earlier they would not. Here too, widespread default is self-fulfilling and with no natural checks. Deflation inevitably follows.

All three deflation mechanisms—the Fisherian, the Minskyian, and the Bernankian—use the idea of the fallacy of composition to identify deflation's self-generating quality. All three approaches begin with an overhang of debt; it is rational for any one individual to pay down his or her debt, but it is self-defeating when everyone wishes to do the same. It is the latter that is the cause of deflation and also what keeps it entrenched there.

It would then be the case that if policymakers can control the scale of financial system distress through the sort of measures the U.S. Fed, the Bank of England, and the ECB have recently adopted, we should succeed in averting deflation. Keynes's fear that monetary policy would prove ineffective as the central bank rate approached zero—his liquidity-trap argument that at zero percent the opportunity cost of money is zero and so money has lost all its power to signal risk—will have been answered. Today's central bankers would reply to Keynes that, yes, that may be so, but we have expanded our balance sheets and become the counterparty to whichever financial institution needs to trade its assets—and at prices that reflect risk as determined by the central bank—and that keeps the credit channels open. Furthermore, central banks have expanded their box of tools to include credit policy in addition to monetary policy, especially when monetary policy has allegedly lost its effectiveness when interest rates have dropped to near zero. Hence, central bankers would now claim, there is no need for panicky early settlement of debts and liquidation of businesses. These economists would be entitled to say they have discovered a powerful tool against deflation risk (Figure 8.1).

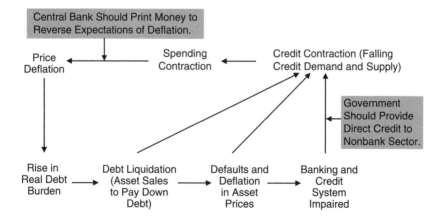

FIGURE **8.1 Debt Deflation Process and Government Intervention Options**

But, seen from the perspective of the SuperCycle, one should not be at all impressed. When one mentions the Bank of Japan's adoption of unorthodox measures, first a zero-interest-rate policy (ZIRP) starting in 1999 and then quantitative easing—where the central bank flooded the banking system with reserves in the hope that it would be a powerful stimulant to lending—beginning in 2001, it only invites mirth or disdain from Fed officials. There is a (publicly) unspoken belief that the Japanese may be good at making cars, but they are poor at any kind of macroeconomic management. The Fed, we are told, is doing more than quantitative easing; it is unclogging the plumbing in the U.S. financial system by taking illiquid assets off the banks' balance sheets.

Yet it is the Japanese central bank's ZIRP that I wish to focus on because it is more relevant to our discussion on deflation. As the authorities pushed the call money rate (the Japanese policy rate) down to zero, deflation became rooted in its economy. *In fact, deflation became worse the longer the call money rate stayed at zero.* So even as the nominal call money rate remained at zero, the *real* call money rate rose to 1.5 percent in 2000 and then 2.0 percent in 2002. At the time of this writing, the U.S. central bank has had a ZIRP in place for several months. The U.S. authorities would do well to heed the Japanese experience.

Here's why. We customarily think of real rates as being the difference between nominal rates and past (or sometimes expected) inflation. In other words, nominal rates and inflation are the independent variables, and the level of real rates (being the difference between those two) is the dependent variable. However, as the nominal rate gets close to zero, the real rate ceases to be dependent, and it swaps places with inflation, which then becomes the dependent variable. In other words, real rates become "fixed" at some positive level as nominal rates get down to zero. And since inflation is the dependent variable, it means inflation becomes negative—that is, we get deflation. This must seem so counterintuitive to the reader that it borders on the outrageous. Why and how could it work that way?

In a highly indebted economy where debt forgiveness is—perhaps for political reasons—inconceivable, the authorities will typically use forbearance to heal the economy and so repair the financial system. This means that monetary policy in particular will be pressed aggressively in the service of stimulating the economy, and rates will go as far down as necessary and perhaps even further. Although this may cause some steepening of the yield curve—that is, the gap between long-term and short-term yields widens—in fact, in a highly risk averse environment long-dated yields come down as well. This was certainly the case in Japan when the 10-year Japanese government bond (the JGB) breached 1 percent at various points when the overnight call money rate was at zero. In our current climate, where the debt is domestically held—that is, where creditors are taking no currency risk—the market begins to expect a positive "real" rate on so-called risk-free assets, that is, assets with the full backing of the sovereign authority. The only way that is possible when nominal rates, regardless of maturity, are unusually low is by making inflation negative.

And this is the way it actually happens. When banks have government backing and they are borrowing at close to government rates but are also being "coerced" to lend at rates that are lower than they would otherwise demand for the risk of default—and, remember, this happens when the central bank, like the U.S. Fed these days, sets the price on the assets it buys from the banks—they begin to impose "quantity" restrictions on lending. This means that banks will impose a necessarily higher degree of creditworthiness standards (typically a higher operating cash flow) on their borrowers so that the demand for credit is curbed until it meets the reduced supply of it—periodically reflected in the U.S. banking system through the

Fed's survey of lending standards. Since labor costs are usually the largest expense component in any business, managers will look to prune those. However, labor markets tend to be inflexible in many places, and by that I mean it is either hard to lay off workers because of worker-protection laws or because severance and rehiring costs tend to be prohibitively high. Even in the more flexible labor markets—the manufacturing sector in Japan and much of the U.S. economy—it is often easier to cut nominal wages. This is the start of wage deflation, and once wage deflation gets under way, a more generalized form of price deflation follows.

The point of this long and rather unusual explanation of deflation is that there are hidden dangers in following the course of action that the Fed has held in reserve and that it seems to have hinted at in some of its statements in early 2009—that it could keep policy rates at close to zero for a long period of time. Put simply, the danger is this: when an overhang of debt is a serious problem in an economy, a super-easy monetary policy paradoxically produces the precise outcome that the policy is designed to thwart. Put another way, very low nominal rates cannot be used to fight deflation, since they are, in these conditions—the conditions of banking system distress—the cause of deflation. I call this the **Paradox of the Zero Bound.**

Yet the tragedy of the situation is that the obverse does not hold. Rising nominal rates do not forestall deflation. Once rates are lifted off rock-bottom levels, the old relationship between nominal and real rates returns: real rates become the difference between nominal rates and inflation. Raising nominal rates thus chokes off the recovery because real rates rise with them. This is the situation Japan has found itself in for much of this past decade, an unrelenting stagnation. The trick is to somehow bring inflation in by other means; and that is where we now turn our attention.

THE LIGHTNESS OF INFLATION

Toward the end of Section III we explained how the U.S. economy shook off the effects of the Classical SuperCycle, which had ended so catastrophically with the Great Depression. Leaving the Gold Standard behind, economists and policymakers rediscovered the power of monetary and, especially, fiscal policy as a means for stabilization when an economy is in free fall. But there was a price to be paid for it. The public debt soared in the 1940s, and yet borrowing rates were constrained. Inflation eroded the real value of the debt, though unlike the 1970s inflation, it did not embed itself into the economy. This allowed the government as debtor to inflate away its own debt. Will the central bank here in the U.S. economy—and in other places where fiscal stimulus has been used aggressively—allow public debt to be monetized?

Unless fiscal discipline succeeds in moving the primary budget balance—that is, the government budget *excluding* interest payments—into a surplus, the public debt will "cascade," a term economists use to denote a faster expansion of the debt relative to the country's GDP. The primary budget surplus must be at least equal to the interest payments for the stock of public debt to be stabilized and must be greater than it for the stock to be gradually reduced. Inflation in tandem with artificially low borrowing rates then becomes an irresistible temptation. And if the theory I have advanced here that deflation is *caused* by ultralow policy rates and *not solved* by them, then the argument for making the central bank behave "irresponsibly" becomes attractive. This means monetizing the fiscal deficit and quietly adopting a campaign of noble lies—publicly avowing a commitment to price stability while turning one's back on it in practice. The government may also not have a choice.

It is only the steeliest central bank that will be able to resist the pressure of the political order to limit interest rate increases relative to inflation; in other words, most central banks will find it hard to resist pressure to keep real interest rates negative for a long time. The SuperCycle's logic has driven us to the point where the monetary standard—Enlightened Fiat money—that has reigned largely unchallenged for the last three decades will now be dethroned. The caretaker of that standard, the modern central bank, is seen by many as basing its practices on a devalued repository of knowledge. It was not only unable to stop the recent crisis; it failed to see it coming. These once-venerated institutions remain on the defensive in all the crisis-afflicted economies and acutely vulnerable to political suasion.

How would the present-day economy function with inflation? Will we see a repeat of the late 1940s—where inflation spiked but then came down relatively quickly—or will it be more like the 1970s, which it required the Volcker Fed's shock therapy and structural reform of labor practices of the Carter and Reagan administrations to cure it?

If there is any truth to my assertion that the Enlightened Fiat money system has been maimed by this crisis, then the parallels with the breakdown of the Bretton Woods system and the currency and monetary disorder in the seventies are much stronger than with the post–World War II era. In that earlier period the currency system had just got started amid a sense of optimism that the best of the old Gold Standard system had been revived with the full backing of the United States, and with restraints on the flow of capital. Those ingredients are missing now just as they were missing in the 1970s. But the differences with the seventies are not minor. This time we *want* inflation, which is not something we did then; and so we may need to construct a *sustainable system of indexation.*

In simple terms, indexation entrenches inflation into the economic system but removes the volatility that inflation infuses into expectations; therefore, indexation removes volatility from financial contracts. So wages, pensions, and interest payments on debt pay out according to a formula that is linked to inflation. By doing this we put the U.S. economy—and other economies that are faced with excess debt—on a life support system. We are cleansing the worst effects of the SuperCycle in its terminal phase—the crushing weight of debt accumulated from an excess of exuberance (the household sector), arbitrage and blind ideology (the financial sector), or necessity (the government sector).

Such a system of indexation should come only after a short, sharp burst of unanticipated inflation that reduces the real value of debt. This would be an alternative to keeping rates artificially low as was the case in the post–World War II period. Indexation will then need to be introduced for the reasons stated above. Here is a fuller explanation: after experiencing unanticipated inflation, people become leery about future inflation. As they negotiate financial contracts ex ante, they will start to build in estimates about what that future inflation might be. To play safe, they will build in a margin of error on the upside, so that they do not underestimate inflation. Because different people will have different expectations of future inflation, an element of volatility will be introduced into the actual inflation. This volatility in turn will beget further uncertainty, and new financial contracts will reflect a still higher safety margin.

As we learned in Section I, one of the bedrock ideas of the modern central bank and the standard of Enlightened Fiat money is creating a nominal anchor for everyone's inflation expectations. The central banks had hoped they had found a way of "unifying" inflation expectation. Once this compact is shattered, disorder follows. Indexation is not a new anchor, and it does not unify inflation expectations; it simply makes them irrelevant.

Let's summarize what we have so far. Inflation is needed to lower the real value of debt, but there is a risk that it will create volatile inflation expectations. Indexation helps to neutralize that volatility. But the inflation spike hasn't just affected the value of debt; it has also eroded the real value of wages. Since consumption in the traditionally consumption-heavy economies should not be allowed to collapse—which it would if the price of goods and services rose while nominal wages stayed the same—indexation also becomes a way to restore at least some of the purchasing power lost by households.

The reader would be right to point out that I am being reckless by implying that inflation accompanied by indexation would be the answer to our problems. So let me make myself clear on that point: I am saying no such thing. I am proposing simply a *temporary* solution to reach the needed relative price adjustment of about 20 percent—a very approximate figure—between goods and services, including nominal wages in the services sector, that the logic of the SuperCycle drives us inexorably toward. It is quite possible that the system of indexation will be little more than a flimsy thing against full-blown and accelerating inflation. But the important thing is, it buys us time: inflation's whiff is first picked up in the commodity markets, transmitted to the goods market, and only then does it reach services and the services-heavy economies, like that of the United States, that have threatened to cripple the world economy. A surge of inflation roaring up the pipeline—in effect, a fast-motion reversal of the whole 30-year SuperCycle process—would hit U.S. households with devastating consequences. The U.S. consumer will not be able to absorb a terms-of-trade turnaround without some degree of protection. Indexation does that.

Without a doubt, inflation will infest an anchorless world. This is the downward spiral of the SuperCycle, the unraveling of it. If the SuperCycle is the process of rolling deflations traveling through the pipeline leaving booms and busts in its wake, the return of inflation marks the undoing of SuperCycle. Rather like vegetation that overruns the physical environment in the absence of humans, inflation reclaims the economic environment as its primordial domain. The wheel of misfortune will then turn again, and we will begin our search for the next monetary standard.

POLICY CONFUSION AND STAGFLATION

In an ideal world, we should find a way to distribute the load that the SuperCycle leaves us with. I'm referring to creating a system with a self-correcting mechanism in it, so that the full weight of forbearance—the healing of the debt-afflicted sectors by stimulating growth—is borne not just by aggressively countercyclical monetary and highly expansionary fiscal policies (which we know create their own set of problems) but by different points on the SuperCycle. I am arguing, in effect, for creating a third policy pillar for achieving stabilization. I call this *involution*, which is best imagined as taking a long sock and pulling the inside out, then opening the closed end and sewing up the open end. If we see the SuperCycle as being something like this sock, then involuting it means turning it inside out so that net producers of goods will now become net consumers; and vice versa. Such a pillar would be built on changes to exchange rates and the use of inflation—high inflation in the new producer economies and still higher inflation in the new consumer-driven economies—so as to make it worthwhile for such a reversal of roles to be effected. This is, of course, an idealized framework that takes me outside the scope of this book and so I will leave it at that.

In the more realistic outcome though, policymakers in the major debtor economies will stay with our conventional two-pillar strategy of partially monetizing fiscal deficits, therefore reluctantly admitting some inflation into the system. Suspicion of indexation—because it smacks of accepting inflation as something permanent—means that inflation will exhibit some volatility. At the same time we cannot expect long-term market-determined interest rates in the U.S. and U.K. economies to be any more controlled than, say, food will be rationed. Hence, both nominal and ex post real rates will enter a period of volatility.

The turmoil in the U.S. bond markets that will likely follow will be reminiscent of the bear market in bonds in 1994, though hardly as short-lived as that one. It may be a period more akin to the 1970s, which were characterized by several bear markets. This time, though, the behavior of the U.S. dollar will be critical. If U.S. inflation is running higher than inflation elsewhere, the U.S. dollar will be appreciating in real terms. This will put U.S. policymakers in a fatal bind: should they attempt to talk down the dollar—since exports could be the main channel for output recovery and so a means of forbearance—or should they talk up the currency as a way of countering the mounting aversion of foreign buyers of U.S. debt who will by this time be demanding higher yields on their holdings?

The result of this policy confusion will be alternating periods of inflation and stagnation, and sometimes mild forms of both at the same time—stagflation. The temptation for policymakers to be conventionally wrong rather unconventionally right—in Keynes's famous words—means that they will adopt measures that make this a likely outcome.

Next we will examine the sort of investments that should go into our portfolios if any of these three scenarios come about.

· CHAPTER 9 ·

Investment Portfolio Implications

F inancial markets have endured one of the most turbulent episodes in history. At the time of first col-
lecting data for this book in late February 2009, the
peak to trough fall in the S&P 500 since the start of the
credit crunch stood at over 50 percent. A collapse of that
magnitude surpasses the bursting of the dot-com bubble,
the crash of 1987, and the OPEC crisis of 1973. We have
to go as far back as the 1930s to find a more acute equity
sell-off. It is not surprising that a fascination with the Depression era has developed and concerns over deflation for
a while replaced the inflation scare that prevailed in the
first half of 2008. Yet inflation worries have never quite
gone away, as evidenced by the behavior of commodity
prices and especially gold.

Investment strategists have recently been asking themselves
whether deflation or high inflation is the more harmful to asset
class performance, and to which asset class in particular. In this
chapter, we will survey asset class and equity sector performance
across inflation and deflation regimes since the 1920s.

At various points over the past six years (2002 to 2008),
the distribution of returns in bonds but especially in equities

has moved around quite a bit: sometimes imitating—or at least anticipating—a period of inflation, sometimes as if we were sliding into deflation, and sometimes stagflation. Although I have dismissed the notion of benign or good deflation, the market does not share my skepticism because it works off a different theory and a different frame of reference. (You, the reader, who has persisted this far should now decide whether my approach is a worthier one.) For purposes of investment strategy, it might be useful to distinguish between phases of (ostensibly) good and (unquestionably) bad deflation to gain further insight and find that, in fact, deterioration in credit conditions often precede bad deflation, and so this may be a useful factor to consider in determining trends in equities. However, we will not push forward too far in that direction since much of my effort in the earlier part of the book has been to prepare us for an unwinding of the SuperCycle—and hence the arrival of inflation, which is where our attention should be directed.

But before we do that, let us take a historical perspective on the remarkably resilient intellectual trends that motivate tilts in strategic asset allocation toward one asset class or another—sometimes with commodities treated as an asset class as well.

PERSISTENCE OF INTELLECTUAL TRENDS

There have been two clear periods when equities were preferred to bonds and just one when the opposite was true. In each case the preference for one asset class over the other was so deeply rooted that it seemed as if the adherents exhibited cultlike characteristics—as wittily noted by Barclays Capital chief investment strategist, Timothy Bond. In each case the beliefs emerged from a redefinition of the most visible risk or return qualities of the asset class in question. This chapter draws on the fundamental work of Barclays strategists and the data collected by Barclays Global Investors—now part of the BlackRock investment management product family—to create a taxonomy of asset class performance in a variety of different macroeconomic conditions.[1]

U.S. investors were the first to start to think seriously about the broad investment policy question of how to allocate funds between stocks and bonds. It was the singular contribution of Edgar Lawrence Smith, whose legendary book *Common Stocks as Long Term Investments* is now hardly remembered, who made what was then regarded as a compellingly strong case for equities.[2] His explanation was that higher dividend yields (relative to bond yields) would be immediately captured and that investors undistracted by the short term would also see equity prices appreciate over longer periods of time. He ascribed this factor to the reinvestment of profits into the expansion and organic growth of the underlying business, and also to demographic changes and technological innovation.

But this argument did not survive the events of later in the decade. The Crash of 1929 put an end to equities as a favored asset class. The Great Depression had such a traumatic effect on risk appetite that bonds were the preferred asset class in the United States and United Kingdom for 20 years up until the mid-1950s, never mind that nominal yields were in the low single digits in those same two economies. These yields by the way stayed low not because the economies were still in a slump but because their governments had arbitrarily held yields on their debt low.

Dividend yields in these economies remained substantially higher than government bond yields through much of this period partly because they more accurately reflected a positive return on investment after making allowance for inflation but in part reflecting a lingering belief that the greater risk inherent in equities required a greater real yield in compensation. And this seemed to be borne out by events: equities' actual return performance through much of the 1930s was dismal because price destruction was rampant.

If we simply looked at the first 10 years or so after the Crash of 1929, it made sense for investors to be wary about equities. The asset class's performance had been nothing short of abysmal. Real returns from equities, that is, capital appreciation after reinvestment of dividends, hardly seemed to support assertions from the 1920s equity evangelists about long-run outperformance. In the 10 years to 1939, the average annual real return from U.S. equities was half that of cash (3 percent) and far below the real return from bonds (7 percent). These high real rates are not as odd as they may appear since these are fixed-income paying instruments and they benefited from deflation. But the capping of government bond yields during the war and the immediate aftermath also distorted the equity/bond yield relationship. By 1950, U.S. equity earnings yields were nearly four times as high as government bond yields.

The preference for bonds persisted at a time of occasionally negative real yields on these bonds in the period after World War II. As explained in the previous chapter, the governments in the United States and United Kingdom had monetized some of their stock of debt—through direct central bank financing of the fiscal deficits that were still being run after the war—and the inflation that followed eroded the returns on bonds whose nominal yields were held low by government discretion. But so great was the prestige of the governments of these economies after the Depression and World War II and so low was the standing of private sector borrowers (who were mostly corporations) that the steady erosion of real government bond yields was thought to be acceptable when the alternative was a high risk of default on corporate bonds or uncertain underlying value in the case of equities.

But this was the last time bonds would have the upper hand. Equities would eventually shake off the curse of their association with the Great Depression. They surged ahead—with new intellectual arguments to support their advance—in the 1950s and then got a fresh boost in the 1990s. Given the experience with inflation and negative real yields on bonds in the years after the war, the case for equities was built at least initially on the basis of their salient characteristic as a hedge against inflation— a case that is still a good one and that we shall reinforce later in the chapter. By the late 1950s, dividend yields fell below government bond yields in the U.K. financial markets as equity prices moved up, and this rationalization enjoyed widespread appeal. Similar developments took place in the United States.

If we had to narrow down the specific period when the equity culture found a wind at its back, it would be the years from 1956 to 1959. This period can be seen as marking the coming of age of equities as a widely accepted asset class for the systematic investors. Investment practice came to recognize that the capacity for future profit growth provided investors with a recompense for the higher risk of owning equities. We have already mentioned that profit growth was seen as providing a better inherent hedge against inflation than fixed-rate bonds. Long-term investors, whose lengthy holding horizon provided an ability to disregard the higher volatility of equities over the short term, were seen to be well placed to extract these benefits. Put differently, the higher risk that we associate with an asset that exhibits high price volatility falls away when we extend our time horizon. We were now being told to overlook the day-to-day or week-to-week or month-to-month volatility, but to focus on equities' potential to deliver steady long-term capital gains. (It was really the same argument that had been put forth by Edgar Lawrence Smith, but this time it was couched in the language of securities analysis.)

This especially appealed to institutional investors, such as the then widely prevailing defined benefit funds. For the hedging of a liability that falls due in 20 or 30 years, what matters is the total return over the period, not the isolated return generated in any single year. The net result of this philosophical shift was a fall in forecasted risk premium on equities versus bonds, and the dividend yield ratio dropped below long-term government bond yields as pension and insurance funds increased equity weightings at the expense of bonds.

The equity culture lasted 40 years and survived the hammer blows of inflation and then stagflation in the 1970s somewhat better than bonds. Of course, some investment strategists would dispute the assertion that equities were preferred to bonds during the years of inflation. It could be the case that ex post equities held up better than fixed income, but it does not follow from that that ex ante equities were the favored asset class. There is no way of resolving this dispute other than to go back to that period and see surveys of how institutional investors planned to allocate their funds; but since asset allocation was a fledgling and hardly publicized activity, such an effort would likely not turn up conclusive results. I prefer, therefore, to see this second period of equity domination—where stocks were seen by asset allocators as being less risky over long periods of time and therefore undervalued by markets—as a largely unbroken 40-year stretch that came to a peak in the tech bubble of the late 1990s.

But this orthodoxy was unquestionably under challenge after the tech bust. Unsurprisingly, in the wake of the equity market bubble and bust, perceptions regarding the riskiness of equities became pronounced. The historical return differential between stocks and bonds for the half century before 2005 did not support equities as the undervalued asset class, or the asset class that was better able to preserve values in a changing economic environment.

Over 10 years between 1995 and 2005, U.K. equities delivered returns of 64 percent, while a portfolio of the United Kingdom's risk-free government bonds returned 88 percent. (These calculations are courtesy of the former Barclays Global Investors team, now part of the BlackRock group.) This comparison gets much worse when we extend the period to the end of the first quarter of 2009, when equity returns had dropped by a *further* 25 percent, and U.K. government bonds gave further positive returns of close to 20 percent. But even so the out-performance of bonds in the last few years has been if not too short-lived then certainly too erratic for anyone to say that the cult of the equity is dead and the cult of fixed income, particularly government bonds, has returned.

We are now in a transitional period. Why do I call it transitional? Not because we know what we are transitioning to but because the economic and market conditions today bear the signature of earlier periods, some in which bonds did well and some in which stocks outperformed. In short, the possibilities are numerous and we await resolution.

Bonds have been the favored asset class for much of the first decade of this century, largely due to the outperformance of developed-country government bonds. (In globally benchmarked portfolios that minimize the inclusion of emerging-market equities, this is still more the case.) Yet there is no conviction that this will be so. In the attempt to establish some relationship between those conditions and the relative performance of the broad asset classes, it is time now to look at these broader economic conditions and to do so without regard to what culture was prevalent.

SCENARIO IMPLICATIONS

We begin our review of scenario implications by examining the average real returns of U.S. equities, bonds, and cash during three separate periods of history. First, we will look at the stable years when inflation ran between 0 and 4 percent. Next, we'll examine the three high inflationary phases since 1929. High inflation is classified as inflation greater than the long-run average of 4 percent. Finally, we'll review the years of deflation when the annual inflation rate was negative. Table 9.1 provides the reader with more specific details on asset class performances, though it combines bonds—both issued by government and corporate entities—into a single asset class. Furthermore, it also includes commodities' performance as an investment. In our explanation of investment performance in the next couple of pages, however, we treat government, or risk-free, bonds as separate from corporate bonds.

TABLE 9.1 **U.S. Asset Returns by Business Cycle Quadrant, 1929 to 2008**

Nominal Yearly Returns Since 1929

Regime	Equity	Bonds	T-Bills	Commodities
Low GDP, low CPI	14.9	9.6	3.1	3.8
High GDP, low CPI	13.3	7.7	3.7	2.5
High GDP, high CPI	13.7	3.3	3.9	28.2
Low GDP, high CPI	4.0	1.0	4.6	25.0

Real Yearly Returns Since 1929

Regime	Equity	Bonds	T-Bills	Commodities
Low GDP, low CPI	14.0	9.3	2.9	0.4
High GDP, low CPI	10.6	5.2	1.3	-0.8
High GDP, high CPI	8.4	-1.4	-1.0	21.7
Low GDP, high CPI	-1.9	-5.0	-1.7	13.7

Nominal Yearly Returns Since 1986

Regime	Equity	Bonds	T-Bills	Commodities	No. of Observations
Low GDP, low CPI	14.1	14.4	3.4	4.7	6
High GDP, low CPI	15.6	10.8	4.6	-3.9	5
High GDP, high CPI	13.6	6.1	4.9	23.4	9
Low GDP, high CPI	-6.4	6.4	7.7	34.9	1

Real Yearly Returns Since 1986

Regime	Equity	Bonds	T-Bills	Commodities	No. of Observations
Low GDP, low CPI	11.4	11.8	1.0	2.3	6
High GDP, low CPI	13.4	8.7	2.6	-5.8	5
High GDP, high CPI	9.7	2.4	1.3	19.1	9
Low GDP, high CPI	-11.8	0.3	1.5	27.1	1

Source: Adapted from Barclays Capital, The Barclays Capital Global Equity Gilt Study 2008, *London, February 13, 2008.*

PERIODS OF INFLATION

Stocks produce the best returns during periods of low and stable inflation with an average real return of 11 percent. Yet when it is neither, as the Barclays studies show, the short-term performance can be poor; on closer examination we see that equities experience declines in the face of *unexpected* inflation spikes. We see that especially clearly in U.S. stocks, which slumped in 1973 to 1974 before rallying the following year. But if we take an overall view and do not break up inflation periods into those years when inflation is anticipated and those when it is not, we note that equities produced a small positive average real return during these periods. Another pattern also soon presents itself: the positive equity returns come mainly from natural resource companies.

How do bonds do in this low-inflation world? As one would expect, government and corporate bonds did well in this environment, though not as well as stocks. During the low and stable inflation years, credit spreads barely moved with an average spread change of half a basis point (0.005 percentage points).

During the deflationary years, stocks provided the worst performance, with poor returns across all the sectors. Instead, returns were concentrated in government bonds and cash as both perform well, as they do traditionally, during periods of risk aversion. Credit spreads, that is, yield spreads of corporate over government bonds, on the other hand, widened quite dramatically during deflationary episodes. As we'll see, the deflationary years show an average spread change of 1 percentage point or 100 basis points during all deflationary periods since 1929.

The high inflation periods are poison for government bonds, especially since the practice of indexing bond coupons to the inflation rate is growing but still not widespread in the developed world—as we will discuss a little later in this chapter when we come to "tilting" portfolios to gain from inflation. As in a low inflation world, equities recover after the initial shock of unanticipated inflation, though their performance is less favorable than when inflation is low. Interestingly, credit spreads on corporate bonds did not do too badly, suggesting that in some respects corporate bonds behave more like equities than like their risk-free counterparts.

Thus, in immoderate conditions of deflation or high inflation, portfolio diversification does not seem to be the best approach given that returns are so heavily concentrated in either resource-based stocks in the case of inflation, or government bonds in the case of deflation.

PERIODS OF DEFLATION AND STAGFLATION

To put the more recent inflation experience in context, we'll next compare sector behavior during the past five years with sector behavior during the deflationary episode in the 1930s and the stagflationary episode in the 1970s. Here and in the next subsection, I draw on the findings of Barclays' asset allocation research that has examined these patterns more closely than anyone else. We separate the equity returns over the past six years into two phases: the first phase covering 2003 to July 2007 to capture the period of global growth and booming equity and commodity markets, which originally led to the inflation scare, and the second phase covering the credit crunch until early 2009. There is an impressive similarity between the sector returns of the 1970s and the 2003 to 2007 period. In both cases, the commodity-driven inflation spike led to portfolio returns being highly concentrated in commodity-related equity sectors. There also appears to be some similarity between sector returns during the Great Depression and the credit crunch. Financials were the worst performing in both cases. Although the current crisis is, as I have argued, a post–Great Depression phase of the SuperCycle—the substantial global fiscal and monetary stimulus currently employed is likely to prevent such an outcome—it is, however, very interesting to note that over the past decade, equity returns have switched from imitating one extreme episode of history to the opposite extreme.

As the preceding chapters have indicated, the greater risk— if that is the right word, since I argue that it is an outcome policymakers must aggressively embrace to save us from more trouble—is that we will have a large dose of inflation in store for us. With that in mind, I wish to focus on recommendations on how to prime portfolios for an inflation-driven environment.

MANAGING INFLATION IN PORTFOLIOS

Inflation is thought to be highly destructive to financial assets because it causes the real value of *fixed* income streams that bonds throw off to decline. Investors react to the loss of income after adjusting for inflation by demanding higher nominal income streams. In simple terms, what this means is that after the appearance of unanticipated inflation, investors want the old level of *real* income to be restored on the assumption that inflation will persist. The only way they can ensure this happens is by demanding a hitherto higher level of *nominal* income. But since bonds—or, at any rate, most bonds—have a fixed coupon, the old bonds must now be discounted in price to make them as appealing as the new bonds issued with the higher coupons. Yet despite all these adjustments during inflationary periods, equities still tend to fare better than bonds because increases in corporate profits can provide some—if not all—of the extra required income, and these adjustments happen naturally, since top line revenue growth is dependent on the sale of products, which automatically reflect inflation.

Falls in equity values during inflationary periods therefore tend to be temporary, whereas falls in bond prices persist until the inflation has subsided. Thus bonds underperform equities during inflationary periods. By illustration, between 1970 and 1980, U.K. equities eked out a cumulative real return of 3.9 percent, a miserable performance that was nevertheless a distinct improvement on the 31 percent loss sustained by government bond investors.

If short-term financial asset returns are negatively correlated with inflation, subsequent long-term returns are positively correlated with inflation. Inflationary periods tend to be temporary. When inflation eventually declines, financial asset yields also decline, boosting total returns. Barclays strategists have demonstrated that the strongest real returns from a mixed portfolio of U.K. stocks and bonds have accrued from starting points of very high inflation by comparing rolling 15-year real returns from a theoretical 60/40 U.K. equity/bond portfolio with the inflation rate at the start of each 15-year rolling period. The broad point is that short-term stock and bond returns are negatively correlated with inflation, while long-term returns are positively correlated with the rate of inflation at the start of any holding period. In the long-run scheme of things, high inflation periods are buying opportunities for both stocks and bonds.

So one way to gain from inflation is to use the elevation in bond or earnings yields as a buying opportunity. In accordance with that, our first lesson is to maintain very high levels of liquidity—partly to thwart negative coincident returns and partly to bargain hunt among depressed assets.

A notable feature of investing during inflation periods is that diversification does not work. Let us look at real returns of a theoretical portfolio that many investment strategists employed in the 1970s: investing 5 percent in cash, 15 percent in commodities, 50 percent in equities, and 30 percent in bonds. Running the numbers looking back at the actual performance of these asset classes, we realize the portfolio performed poorly. In the first seven years of the decade, the portfolio loses a cumulative 30 percent and is still down 5 percent by the end of the decade, according to these ex post calculations done by Tim Bond and other Barclays strategists.

Hence the second lesson for asset allocation in years of inflation is to avoid diversification and focus investment on the handful of assets that benefit from inflation. In practical terms, this suggests a focus on the resources that are causing inflation—reinforcing the case for the inclusion of physical commodities in portfolio allocations.

Of course, there are limits to what history can teach us. Once again these strategists have looked at U.K. and U.S. equity returns by sector during the 1970s (United Kingdom from end-1969, United States from end-1973). Again, the message is the same—positive total returns were concentrated in a couple of sectors that were direct beneficiaries of inflation. We note that basic materials did poorly as a sector in the 1970s. Oil prices vastly outperformed industrial metals and other commodity prices in the 1970s. During the commodity run-up in the inflation scare of 2006 and 2007, oil outperformed some, but not all, other commodities. The lesson we should take away from this is that the weak returns from basic resources during the 1970s might not be the exact template for the period we could be entering at the time of this writing. Overall, in both equity markets only the oil and gas and industrials sectors provided positive real returns during the 1970s.

However, we can draw a general lesson here. So another—our third—lesson for active asset allocation in inflation years is to be overweight in energy, industrial goods (and—in current markets—basic resources), and equity sectors against under-weights in consumer goods and services, as well as in health care, utilities, telecoms, and technology.

Although equity returns failed to fully hedge inflation during the 1970s (which we must remember was not strictly a period of continuously low or high or even predictable inflation, but one of stagflation characterized by variable inflation rates), this was attributable more to widespread derating—that is, a lower-ing of the ratio of stock price to earnings—than to really weak growth in earnings. In fact, in both the United Kingdom and the United States, earnings outpaced inflation by a small margin during the decade. Since, as we have pointed out earlier, a key component of corporate profits is output pricing, it is rational for profit growth to track inflation.

In the 1970s, investors could access corporate earnings only via the medium of standard equity investments. Today, it has become possible to access the corporate profit stream some-what more directly via the medium of dividend swaps—invest-ing in the dividend stream alone rather than the dividend plus the book value plus market capitalization of the long-run flow of dividends.

The historical record is mixed when we try to analyze the success of such a dividend-only strategy during the last great inflation in the 1970s. This is because those equity sectors whose earnings would have provided the most effective infla-tion hedge during the 1970s also cut their payout ratios the most. Aggregate market dividend payout ratios fell during the decade. Thus the S&P 500 payout ratio fell from 54 percent at the end of 1969 to 40 percent at the end of 1980. A comparable fall is visible in the U.K. payout ratio, which declined from 64 percent in 1969 to 44 percent at the end of 1980.

However, the 1970s experience with dividends is probably not a very useful guide to the current era. This is because dividend payout ratios were exceptionally high at the end of the 1960s (56.3 percent in the first quarter 1970), while they are historically low at present.

If we examine 1970s returns from dividends only, starting our analysis after payout ratios had moderated somewhat, we find that dividend payments tend to outpace inflation. We also find that dividend-only total returns beat equity total returns by a reasonable margin.

So unless we assume an improbable decline in dividend payout ratios from existing low levels, it is reasonable to suggest that dividend-only investments should outperform total equity investments if the current inflation environment is sustained over the medium to long term. So the fourth lesson we should take away from the years of inflation—although once again cautioning ourselves not to read too much into the similarities of that period with ours—is to prefer dividend-only investments to complete equity exposure.

In the 1970s, the index-linked market did not exist. Today, there is a global inflation-linked government bond market totaling over $1.5 trillion with 23 different sovereign borrowers, including all members of the G-7 and a number of developing nations. Alongside the government markets there is a large inflation-linked derivatives and options sector. Investors now have the option of investing directly in inflation (breakevens and inflation swaps) or in a mix of inflation and real returns (straight long position in an index-linked bond). Although the inflation-linked bond market has grown rapidly over the past few years, the asset class is generally underrepresented in portfolios. This is the fifth lesson, namely, that we include index-linked securities.

The final way to gain from inflation is the riskiest, but the gains are potentially the greatest. In the decade of the 1970s, the price of gold rose from $35 to over $600. After accounting for inflation, gold delivered an eightfold real return during the inflationary 1970s. However, during the first two years of the disinflation trend (1980 and 1982), gold prices more than halved to trade just above $300, which, as we have noted in the main part of the book, is one of the most compelling demonstrations of the SuperCycle at work. Oil, in comparison, had fallen from $37 to $34 over the same period. Gold certainly has a small role in inflation-tilted portfolios, but its extreme volatility suggests the role should remain modest.

LIMITS TO HISTORY

We should take history as a guide, but only a rough one. The SuperCycle's future trajectory is truly unknown. A more extreme kind of stagflation—a hyperstagflation, for example—will test the usefulness of all our observations and intuitions about tactical portfolio adjustments, never mind our theories, which are already suspect. So, I end on this ambivalent note. Everything I know about the workings of the SuperCycle tells me that the future will be turbulent; yet our investment portfolios have the capacity to be flexible, and we will be spending rather more time than we have in the past tending to them.

Minsky's and Koo's Challenges to the Dominant Theory

We could consider instead the most popular alternative explanation for financial crises (identified most closely with Hyman Minsky and his followers—and some of Minsky's forebears such as the late Prof. G. L. S. Shackle, a British economist—though I present it here in a more general form, which owes at least as much to the recent work of others). There are critical differences between my interpretation of recent economic history and those of the aforementioned economists, but it is worth surveying some of their essential ideas on the destabilizing impulses of modern financial capitalism.

Their explanation asserts that the present crisis is one of collateralized lending in a climate of asset inflation. The structural circumstances that produced the boom and then the crisis were the inflow of credit into asset markets and the reversal of that inflow. These inflows and current outflows were part of the system of collateralized lending that prevailed in the United States and United Kingdom in recent years and in Japan two decades ago. Collateralized lending consists of lending against asset values with little regard to the income generated from the asset or from any other entity that had some sort of contingent responsibility for the creditworthiness of the borrower. This activity is seen initially as providing security for the lending bank, and thus it is considered a less risky form of lending.

When more credit comes into the financial markets than firms and governments are willing to employ by issuing new securities, the prices of existing securities rise. Short-term securities and all bonds usually have the price at which they are repaid written into the terms. As the date of their repayment approaches, their market price converges on their repayment price. The market price of such bonds will exceed that repayment price before maturity by only a small margin reflecting any differences between the interest payable on such a bond and the interest payable on equivalent new issues, as has been explained in Chapter 9. Excess demand for new securities will tend to inflate equities the most since they do not have any fixed repayment value—though not without limit, of course, since they must have some relationship to the value of debt.

Corporations have found from time to time that they could issue shares cheaply because they could issue shares at a high price relative to dividends. Buyers were willing to pay these high prices because they came to expect an additional return in the form of capital gain—not paid by the company, but by future buyers in the market for shares. As a result of excess demand for shares, corporations issued capital in excess of what they needed to finance commercial and industrial operations. This occurred during some big equity market booms, most recently in the U.S. tech sector during the Internet bubble years of the late 1990s, though, as explained in Chapter 7, not in the European technology companies.

In the past, shareholders disapproved of overcapitalization of companies because it diluted earnings per share profits. But when expected returns on investment are far greater than the interest rate on borrowed funds, which in turn is greater than the earnings yield on the company's shares, equity issuance is the most rational form of capital raising.

This excess equity capital, in these cases, has been used in equity booms—both as cause and effect of the boom—to replace bank borrowing with cheaper long-term capital. Replacing borrowing with shares also has the advantage that pretax profits can be made to rise by the reduction in interest cost. Where excess capital has not been used to reduce debt, it has been used to buy short-term financial assets. Alternatively, excess capital is committed to buying and selling companies—hence the merger and takeover activity and balance sheet restructuring that has characterized corporate finance since the 1980s.

In the household sector, the equivalent of financial asset inflation is the inflation of the housing market. The removal of restrictions on housing credit—and indeed the encouragement of mortgage debt—made it much easier for households to obtain credit for house purchases. Increased credit then allowed demand continually to drive up prices, with a temporary relapse in the late 1980s and at the beginning of the 1990s.

As house prices rise, according to these economists, wealth and capital gains are distributed from those entering the housing market, usually on somewhat lower incomes at the beginning of their careers, to those who have owned real estate for a longer period of time. This system not only redistributes income and wealth from the asset poor to the asset rich but it also turns the housing market into a giant Ponzi scheme, a critically important stage in the Minskyian system.

Once rising house prices are taken for granted, those entering the market with huge debts can comfort themselves with the prospect of capital gains if they can survive paying most of their income in debt payments. The political consensus since the 1980s has considered this the only proper solution for securing decent accommodation.

The main stabilizing mechanism operated through the housing market. The rise in the value of real estate and financial assets induced a change in the saving behavior of the middle classes. Hitherto the middle classes saved more or less passively: income was put into savings to support future consumption in retirement. From the 1980s, active use of balance sheets to generate cash flow became much more common among property owners. Asset inflation allowed the emergence of an alternative "welfare state of the middle classes" based on borrowing against rising asset values, or the sale of inflated assets. Borrowing against assets was meant to substitute for income in periods of unemployment. In fact, tapping into assets and turning them into a stream of income was an important underpinning for Ben Bernanke's explanation of forces shaping the now risibly termed Great Moderation.

The more common use of debt or asset sales to pay for current expenditure brought down overall saving rates in the U.K. and U.S. household sectors to negligible or negative levels. According to this school of thought, this stabilizer of housing market–financed consumption broke down from around 2006.

In the housing market, there was clearly a limit on young people's ability, at the start of their careers, to indebt themselves, even with the prospect of capital gains in later middle age. Significantly the housing boom did not implode where houses were most expensive and where capital gains may have been said to be the greatest, and hence where a speculative bubble may have been most distended. Instead, the boom broke where incomes were lowest, in the subprime sector of the market, where the market in the asset was least liquid, and where excessive debt could be serviced only out of a low and unreliable income, rather than capital gain.

With a reduction in credit entering capital and housing markets, relative to credit being taken out of those markets, asset inflation reversed into asset deflation. Collateralized lending now choked off the supply of credit even further. This obliged new purchasers to put more of their own money into house purchases. The higher down payment requirement reduced the number of borrowers capable of meeting the standard for prudent collateralized lending. Moreover, with falling asset values, homeowners found that the excess of collateral value over outstanding loan value disappeared, and it may even have become negative.

In a situation of asset deflation, debt that previously could be written off against relentless capital gain and serviced through what was popularly termed MEW, or mortgage equity withdrawal—which was obtained through home equity loans or through refinancing of mortgages with higher loan-to-value ratios—must then be paid out of income. This development created a problem of excess debt in the economy, which forced households to raise savings rates. While most economists regard all savings as essentially voluntary and hail it as facilitating investment, debt previously serviced out of capital gains but then serviced out of income is a form of "forced saving."

A person forced to service debt out of income in this way will try to reduce this debt, rather than spend income or, in the case of a firm, spend on new equipment. This adverse pattern arises because selling assets cannot pay such excess debt, and its existence on the credit record of a person makes it more difficult to obtain credit in the future.

By reducing current expenditure, asset deflation forced the economy into recession. Recession brought down the rate of inflation, affecting current goods and services (measured by the consumer price index, retail price index, or GDP deflator). There is now an increased danger that prices of current goods and services will start to fall. If they fall, debt deflation will set in, as falling prices increase the real value of debt in the economy.

Inflation in the economy as a whole is the natural, almost benign way of eliminating excessive debt in the economy: as everyone's incomes and prices rise, the real value of debt declines and debt payments become more manageable. The three decades since the 1970s were marked by intensive efforts on the part of central banks to eliminate inflation, but those efforts left no mechanism for eliminating excessive debts.

Asset deflation turns excessive debts into bad debts. This is because lending against expected increases in capital values, where such increases turn out to be greater than actual asset inflation, leaves a margin of loans without security, and it leaves some borrowers without the means to repay loans. In this way, the loss of capital gains has resulted in a deterioration of bank assets and generalized bank failure because there is then mutual suspicion about counterparties, which causes previously reliable interbank lending to dry up.

In this situation, central bank policy is ineffective: lower interest rates cannot stimulate expenditure in a situation of excess debt because of the preference to use any spare liquidity to repay excess debt. Buying assets from banks ("quantitative or credit easing") or recapitalizing them improves the liquidity of bank balance sheets. Yet this cannot make indebted customers borrow. Banks are being reduced to operating as "zombie" banks, which can make payments (under government guarantee) or take deposits (under bank guarantee) but cannot lend because the nonfinancial sector—in this case the household sector—is paying down its debts. Richard Koo, the Tokyo-based economist at the Nomura Research Institute, has argued that no matter how innovative their policy instruments, central banks will fail, and we have no choice but to fall back on government expenditure when an economy is faced with such an outcome.

I have offered this theory as a foil for the dominant paradigm. Not only does it fit the facts better, ex post, it offers testable and falsifiable predictions at every stage of the analysis because it deals with observable and measurable quantities.

But equally important, it offers concrete and tangible solutions to the paralysis at the heart of the credit creation mechanism. For banks to end the paralysis, the impaired assets must be cordoned off or put in a "bad bank"—where mark-to-market (MTM) is waived and some form of a regulatory capital reduction and/or reprieve is allowed. This would remove the pro-cyclical stress on capital, thereby distributing the losses and capital requirements over time.

Looking further ahead, debtors partly need to be relieved of repayment burdens they cannot meet, and creditors need to accept that they will not be repaid in full. Yet this creditor-to-debtor transfer risks igniting depression if it produces major asset foreclosures. Therefore, inflation is a better way to manage the problem. This is where their prescriptions converge with mine.

Monetary policy, they would argue, would quickly need to become much more "credit or leverage aware." Analyzing credit availability and the amount of credit in the system generates a powerful signal to judge whether an asset bubble is forming.

The Neo-Keynesian school, on the other hand, will now admit that monetary policy has distortionary effects on consumption plans, and while it maintains that these are strictly short term and would self-correct, all else being the same, the truth is that asset prices do not stay the same while this is happening. The inflation and eventual deflation of the asset bubble deeply churn the economy, producing dislocations in output and employment. They will argue that central banks should be concerned about increases in the price of specific assets in addition to inflation, and they should adjust monetary policy accordingly.

So all we will get from the dominant school is an "asset-aware" monetary policy. One can already hear the rumbles deep in the bowels of the beast that until we know what the "equilibrium" level of asset prices is, this approach is not practicable. The idea that asset prices often—and in such cases most disastrously—are determined by credit and leverage measures, which are objectively measurable and remain at book value, will of course be disregarded.

The Many Faces of Gold

GOLD SETS THE STANDARD

Britain's move to gold can be traced back to 1774, a full hundred years before the momentum to adopt it as a global monetary system got under way throughout the rest of the world. It was halted during the Napoleonic War years of 1803 to 1815 when, as a wartime measure, cash payments were suspended and the Bank of England was freed from its obligation to convert notes into gold on demand. But immediately at the end of the war years, the de facto gold standard of the late eighteenth century was made de jure by the passage of parliamentary acts leading to the 1819 restoration of the convertibility of notes to gold. By 1821 Britain was legally on the full Gold Standard.

And yet Britain remained in splendid isolation from the rest of the world in its use of gold to back its money. As for the United States' adoption of gold in the 1830s, whatever American historians may say, the facts tell a clear story. For all practical purposes, the United States was in fact operating on a silver standard though it may have paid lip service to the idea of bimetallism. At 15 ounces of silver to 1 ounce of gold, silver so undervalued the latter that gold disappeared from circulation. The United States thus joined France in resisting the allure of gold until much later in the nineteenth century.

It was early in the 1870s that the movement toward gold accelerated as an international standard. Why did this happen? There is one overriding explanation for this development. In the 1850s and 1860s, there was a surge in price and wage inflation for reasons that are explained in more detail later in this appendix. Although Britain had also experienced a spell of inflation, it had come through in better shape than many other countries. The integrity of its monetary system was much admired, and it should be no surprise that admiration turned to envy and then to imitation. This led to calls for an international monetary conference, which was held in Paris in 1867 and which recommended the adoption of a universal gold standard.

There were also good practical reasons: the sheer dominance of the British economy in the world trading system made it difficult for its trading partners to rely on silver, let alone inconvertible paper money. Germany is a case in point. Its currency, the silver thaler, was not acceptable to Britain in the settling of accounts. Germany, with its aspirations of becoming a great power, soon saw the advantage of switching to gold, which it did in 1872. Germany, perhaps gratuitously, insisted that the reparations from France after the Franco-Prussian War of 1870 to 1871 should be indemnified with gold; whatever the wisdom of that demand, it conferred an additional legitimacy to the metal.

There was always the risk that Germany's other important trading partners, the countries of Central and Eastern Europe, all of which were operating on inconvertible paper currency, would find they were unable to transact with Germany. In fact, quite the opposite happened; it hastened their move to gold as well.

Once Germany succumbed, the other major economies fell like dominoes. Holland, crushed between a gold-using Britain and a gold-using Germany, was the first to go. In 1874 it joined what was then fast becoming an international standard. Norway, Sweden, and Denmark followed suit. The Latin Monetary Union—the European followers of bimetallism led by France—feeling the pressure from their Anglo-Saxon neighbors, suspended the minting of silver coins and moved to a "limping" gold standard, in which silver coinage was still legal tender but ceased to be used in larger transactions. Effectively, these economies had moved to the Gold Standard by 1878.

The United States held out for another year and officially did not give up its allegiance to bimetallism until 1900—a link that would plague it during the "Free Silver" movement led by the Populists. But in practical terms it joined the Gold Standard by restoring the convertibility of paper notes to gold in 1879.

And then suddenly there was a slowdown in the spread of gold, and no new national economies joined the Gold Standard through the decade of the 1880s. But the momentum picked up again in the 1890s. Austria joined in 1892. Russia and Japan joined in 1897, and India, by pegging to sterling, joined in that same year as well. The Philippines' peso (by pegging to the U.S. dollar) joined this arrangement in 1900, leading a final burst of entrants: Siam (now Thailand), Ceylon (now Sri Lanka), Argentina, Mexico, Peru, and Uruguay, all in the first year of the new century. By 1900 it would be fair to say the Gold Standard had become the basis of the international monetary system.

As the Gold Standard spread, it created what we, in our modern parlance, would call "network externalities," meaning that it became more valuable the more participants or users it attracted. Modern commercial technology, of course, is rich in examples of self-fulfilling successes: VHS rather than Betamax, Microsoft operating systems rather than the dozens of others. Network externalities are why real success in any system comes with setting standards that force or induce compliance from others. It may not be the best system, but it has unbeatable first-mover advantages. This is what the Gold Standard achieved.

Further efficiencies resulted from the accidental discovery of the multilateral payments system—accidental because it was not foreseen, and its merits were recognized only as the system evolved. The larger the number of countries trading multilaterally, the greater the opportunity for offsetting surpluses and deficits, and thus the smaller the flow of gold needed to achieve overall balance between the countries concerned. It also followed that the smaller the demands placed on the available stock of gold in the trading countries, the less the likelihood of a country's protecting its trade with other countries in order to protect its gold holdings. Put another way, large bilateral imbalances, which would otherwise be cause for concern, tended to be less egregious in a multilateral context. And, of course, once this mitigating factor came into play, it lent powerful support to the growth of trade between countries. In turn, it removed one of the main objections to gold-backed money and gold-backed settlements of trade.

Yet there was something forbidding about the Gold Standard as it was meant to be applied in an international system, and policymakers in the nineteenth century were fully aware of this. It's one thing for Britain or any other country to back its money with gold and so foster confidence in its domestically circulating notes; it's another matter altogether to force a convergence of economies so that the global economy—or the group of countries that had signed on to this standard—acts as a magnet pulling the price of each traded good down to the lowest world price. Since nominal exchange rates were fixed, this could be achieved only by deflation or inflation. Failure to produce at the lowest prevailing price would encourage allocation of resources away from that activity.

This mechanism by which an economy adjusted its imbalances was known as "price-specie-flow," and it was first proposed by the classical economists David Hume, Adam Smith, and John Stuart Mill. Suppose a country developed a current account deficit because of excessive imports and in keeping with the Gold Standard, it had to export gold to the trading partners against whom it ran deficits. The loss of gold would reduce the domestic money supply, since either gold circulated as money domestically or the banking system kept the economy's internal supply of money adjusted to the quantity of its gold reserves. A decrease in the domestic money supply would lead to a decline in prices of goods since less spending with unchanged output meant markets would clear at a lower price level. Lower prices in turn were meant to increase exports and lower imports, the latter since domestic substitutes for foreign goods would become cheaper. In the gold-receiving economy, that is, the one running current account surpluses, the process is reversed. The inflow of gold increases the domestic money supply and raises the prices of goods, which makes the exporting of goods more difficult and the importing of cheaper foreign supplies more attractive.

The price-specie-flow mechanism worked through interest rate changes in the country concerned. In Britain, gold flows led to changes in the "bank rate," the Bank of England's discount rate, and the changes in the rates were themselves automatic and formed part of the adjustment mechanism. That is, if Britain had to pay out gold, the Bank of England's ratio of gold reserves to liabilities (currency and banking system deposits held with the bank) would fall. If this decline persisted, the Bank of England would raise its discount rate to prevent further depletion of its reserves. Such actions would increase interest rates through the financial system and restrict credit. And the reverse would happen if there was a net gold inflow.

The truth, of course, is that this fearsomely harsh system of adjustment was not often put into practice. Policymakers were not the automatons that historians of that era often make them out to be. They recognized that prices and wages were rather more inflexible than was popularly believed and that the adjustment in terms of sacrificed output (or excessive credit and higher inflation) required by the price-specie-flow mechanism where there were persistent deficits (or surpluses) on the current account would be highly punitive or at least disruptive. This is a lesson that should have been learned by those who have recently attempted monetary system experimentation on an ambitious scale, such as Argentina's disastrous experience with full U.S. dollar convertibility from 1991 to 2002, a variant of the price-specie-flow mechanism, using the dollar in place of gold.

There was one factor that played a dominant role in extenuating these effects of gold flows even after allowing for all the benefits gained from the multilateral payments system. The importance of capital movements is entirely neglected by those who associate the Gold Standard with the rigors of the price-specie-flow movement. In fact, the current account balances of many of these countries remained continuously in either deficit or surplus, that is, out of balance persistently, yet the surpluses tended to be recycled overseas to the deficit countries, therefore keeping the whole system reasonably stable. It was tantamount to a cushioning effect, or an automatic support mechanism, provided by long-term credit facilities.

This was possible largely due to the equilibrating role played by Britain in the international economy and the growth and strength of sterling as a proxy for gold ("good as gold") in the multilateral payments system. Britain remained the major trading economy through the entire period of the formation of the Gold Standard—from the 1870s to the early years of the twentieth century—and the most important source of investible funds. Although it maintained a trade deficit through much of this time, it earned a current account surplus by running a very large surplus on its invisibles account.

The invisibles account is the accounts payable versus accounts receivable for services, interest, dividends, and other forms of income repatriation. The current account becomes the sum of the trade and invisibles accounts. Britain dominated the shipping business worldwide, and this "service" was a major source of earning. Besides, its trade surpluses from an earlier era of manufacturing dominance had been so large and had been so shrewdly invested offshore that they provided a strong income stream.

What made sterling so strong and reliable was that chimerical quality that we in an age of fiat money still call "confidence"—though our reference point, until very recently at least, was the confidence in the central bank's sorcererlike ability to maintain price stability (and other objectives like full employment or maximum sustainable output) simply by virtue of its reputation. The confidence that the world trading system had in Britain was that it would be able to convert sterling to gold, if required, at the fixed exchange rates that had held since 1821. This confidence was axiomatic and lay at the heart of sterling's acceptability. It was this symbiotic relationship between sterling and gold—sterling backed by gold at least initially, and then sterling as a surrogate for gold as the trading system became ever more international—that was the linchpin of the system.

Finally, we must recognize as well that even accounting for all the equilibrating sterling flows, the central banks in fact exercised a greater degree of discretion than an austere interpretation of the Gold Standard would have allowed. Even when gold flows actually occurred, the central banks were never so impotent as to adjust monetary supply promptly and in line with the new level of gold reserves. Sustaining domestic activity was accorded a higher level of importance than many realized.

Up to a point, of course; when the U.S. economy tried to subvert the fundamental rules of the Gold Standard by infusions of liquidity, it created panics, as we shall see presently.

POST-WORLD WAR I "DIRTY" GOLD STANDARD

This much is indisputable, that war leads to inflation. The reasons are clear: primarily, the expansion of aggregate demand is not matched by the expansion of supply of goods and services that are needed for consumption and investment. But the persistence of inflation in the countries of Central and Eastern Europe after World War I—with some of them, Germany, Austria, Poland, and Hungary, even experiencing hyperinflation while many others, notably Britain, France, Italy, and the Netherlands, stabilized relatively quickly—means that we should look deeper for an answer to the causes of inflation in postwar economies.

The United States had remained on gold throughout World War I even as others had left at the start of the war. But Britain, France, Italy, the Netherlands, and the Scandinavian countries, along with Japan, Brazil, and Argentina, had joined an informal arrangement that we today would call a U.S. dollar bloc. Officially, all these fiat, that is, not gold backed, currencies were supposed to float against the U.S. dollar, but in fact they were managed in such a way as not to deviate too far from the dollar or from each other. How was this possible? At that time, the United States was the dominant creditor nation, and it recycled its reserves the way Great Britain had done through most of the Gold Standard years. It allowed imbalances in trade—which had become quite distended by this time due to protectionist tendencies still persisting from the prewar years—to be financed with dollar loans. To put it plainly, this was a continuation of the Gold Standard by other means among at least a small group of countries. We could call it the "dirty Gold Standard," and although this arrangement did not last too long, nor did it have widespread applicability, it was a model for the Bretton Woods system that came after World War II.

GOLD EXCHANGE STANDARD

The stabilization of Germany following World War I and its return to the Gold Standard set off a burst of optimism in the restored international system that would glow for the next few years. The First Law of SuperCycle Motion was in full swing again. Britain had moved off the U.S. dollar peg but was allowing sterling to fluctuate only slightly. With the Gold Standard Act of May 13, 1925, Britain was officially on gold again. By early 1926, 39 countries had returned to gold at prewar parity or somewhat devalued (mainly commodity producers who were experiencing rapidly falling prices). France, Italy, and Argentina were the laggards, and they came along in 1928.

That this was hardly the Gold Standard of the prewar (and especially the pre-1900) era hardly seemed to matter. Its true nature would not stand fully revealed until too late. If any evidence is needed of the power of a mere façade in satisfying the collective yearning for stability, it is to be found in the gold exchange standard of the middle and late 1920s. We can now see clearly with the benefit of hindsight that an international monetary system faced by the shortage of gold, and the rather uneven distribution of gold stocks, would be severely hampered. The United States' gold holdings, as a share of total world stocks, had grown from 24 percent in 1913 to 44 percent in 1923, while those in Britain had risen from 3 percent to 9 percent. On the other hand, certain other economies, like Germany, Italy, Russia, and Brazil, had suffered an absolute loss of gold during these years.

Given this shortage of gold, other acceptable means of international payment had to be found to supplement gold. The Gold Exchange Standard—as it was correctly called—was recommended at the Genoa conference in 1922. Under this arrangement, assets in the form of foreign currencies could be counted as part of the country's international reserves. In other words, a country was allowed to stabilize its currency in terms of a foreign currency that was convertible into gold and to hold its reserves in the form of that currency.

It should be apparent to the reader that this increased the fragility of the system. It concerned the manner in which some countries built up their reserves of convertible currencies. In the absence of a current account surplus or of access to long-term borrowing, many countries acquired reserves by borrowing short term. These reserves were acutely vulnerable to shifts in confidence.

How was this different from the original Gold Standard of earlier days when Britain's (but not just Britain's) surpluses would get recycled to deficit countries and so help them avert the harsh adjustments required by the price-specie-flow mechanism? The difference was that the portfolio flows in the 1920s were short term in nature—that is, they were what we, in recent years, have started to call "hot money."

The Barings Crisis of 1890 to 1891 caused by a default on Argentine debt did produce acute aversion to risk on the part of British creditors. But Argentina and the other Latin American economies were able to devalue their currencies since they were not on gold in the 1890s, and so they forestalled the worst consequences for themselves. Yet U.S. policymakers remembered the damage currency devaluations wrought on American commodity producers, and they felt that the adjustments this time—since all the major trading nations were on the Gold Standard—would have to be borne stoically.

GOLD–U.S. DOLLAR STANDARD (OR THE BRETTON WOODS SYSTEM)

The outcome was the Bretton Woods Articles of Agreement in which all currencies were fixed against gold and the U.S. dollar and, so, were fixed against each other. Strictly speaking, they were allowed to move but only in a very small band. In fact, the band was so small we can think of it as being a fixed exchange rate system. Also, technically, one-off adjustments of exchange rates would be sanctioned by the International Monetary Fund (IMF), so some might prefer to call it a "pegged" exchange rate system, but I'll stay here with the more widely accepted term.

Just as important, cross-border capital flows were not forbidden, but restrictions on the availability of foreign exchange to the residents or nonresidents of each country were retained as a guard against the destabilizing effects of capital flight on the country's balance of payments. In fact, the IMF, one of the two monitoring institutions created at Bretton Woods in 1944, expected its members to introduce controls to prevent such capital movements.

Yet there was a widespread desire to maintain what was regarded as the best features of the old Gold Standard system. On the current account—that is, the part of the balance of payments that deals with the flow of goods and material rather than the flow of capital—there were to be no controls on the convertibility of one currency to another; for all intents and purposes, international trade was not to be regulated. The economies of the world were also expected to strive for stability of exchange rates and avoid competitive devaluations. In addition, however, national economies were allowed the autonomy to pursue independent, that is, uncoordinated, monetary and fiscal policies.

So the seeds of contradiction were being sowed, as alluded to in the early part of this appendix. It will have occurred to the reader that only the restrictions on capital movements allowed this precarious system of dos and don'ts to survive. For example: an economy that for its own political imperatives decided to adopt stimulative fiscal and monetary policy while other countries did not would soon face pressures on its current account as its imports would rise faster than its exports. Since this was a system of fixed exchange rates, there was no relief to be found in that direction. The country's reserves would run down, and it would be tempted to borrow, though it would be dissuaded from doing so by the IMF. Instead, the IMF would advise the policymakers in the economy in question to draw on the IMF's pool of "drawing rights"—that is, the pool of foreign currencies that it holds as a supplement to the international reserves held by each country. This pool was dominated by gold and dollars, and other major currencies like the British pound and Deutsche mark had smaller shares.

It would not be relevant to the main purpose of this book to dwell much longer on why the Bretton Woods arrangement never really worked as well as its creators had hoped other than to say that some of it had to do with the reluctance of the European economies to make their currencies fully convertible on the current account. This meant in effect that their currencies were underrepresented in the international reserves of their trading partners and in the IMF's drawing rights, and the dollar ended up being the sole convertible currency.

World trade did expand rapidly *despite* all the restrictions on capital flows, but with the system of fixed exchange rates, imbalances began to appear, as we would expect. We did see this happen during the Gold Standard period—when exchange rates were also fixed—though the reader will remember that Great Britain was essentially playing the same role that the IMF was meant to in this arrangement, but playing it more effectively. The United States was essentially forced to step in and provide its currency as a source of liquidity to solve the imbalances in the system. And just as Britain's surplus position began to slip in the years just before World War I and its currency ceased to be used as a balancing device, here too it was the United States' deteriorating position that marked a turning point.

That turning point came in 1958 when the United States recorded its first annual balance of payments deficit in the post–World War II period. It is the case that the United States ran these deficits in support of the demand for international liquidity, which is a rather dull sounding term for the refusal of other major countries to contribute to the pool of money available to settle imbalances between economies. What this argument was saying was that if the only way the United States could get the rest of the world to keep a multilateral system of trade and payments going was by assuming the role of provider of reserve assets to others and ignoring its own balance of payments position, then that was what the United States would do. Whatever the true explanation, it is undeniable that as the 1960s progressed and the United States continued to run substantial deficits, the problem became one of confidence in the U.S. dollar. This dollar overhang cast doubt on the credibility of the convertibility of dollar to gold at $35 per ounce of gold.

The rest of the story is well known and has been recounted more thoroughly by others, but it is worth pointing out the salient milestones. When this situation could no longer be maintained, the dollar became inconvertible to gold in 1971. This marked the end of the Bretton Woods system. The dollar exchange standard that had been preferred by the leading economies of the world with all its problems of liquidity, adjustment, and confidence came to a messy conclusion, just like the short-lived Gold Exchange Standard of the 1920s and the Classical Gold Standard of the pre–World War I world. What the world had just come through was the failure of a system that the world expected would hold the confidence of all participants. But the inadequacy of the dollar to play the role of the pound sterling of the Classical Gold Standard era was manifest early on. It was surprising the system lasted as long as it had. As a result of its failure, for possibly the first time in recorded history, the world entered an era of freely floating exchange rates and of domestically circulating money that had no backing of any kind of precious metal.

Yet for all stresses and strains that were created in monetary relations, the 30-year period that ran from the start of World War II until 1970 was marked by an absence of panics, of runs on currencies, and of excessive fluctuations in output that so characterized the Gold Standard and that even more have defined our own era. Most of the advanced countries in this period—the members of the Organization of European Economic Cooperation that later was expanded to become the Organization for Economic Cooperation and Development (OECD)—attained high and generally stable rates of growth. Between 1950 and 1960, the United States suffered three recessions, but in only two of them, 1953 and 1958, did the GDP actually contract during the calendar year in question. The mildness of the downturns can be seen in that each setback was followed in the succeeding year by higher than average increases in output. Western Europe recorded equally mild recessions in 1952 and 1958.

From 1960 to 1973 only three countries in the developed world recorded a reduction in GDP: Australia in 1961, Germany in 1967, and the United States in 1970. In each case the decline was a mere fraction of a percentage point, and, in each case, rates of annual growth that were higher than average followed these mild downturns. This is a period that has been closely studied by economists at the OECD and elsewhere ever since. The readily available supply of low-wage labor partly explains this stability phenomenon as does the expansion of the public sector everywhere. An authoritative study of the Western European economies by the economist Michael M. Postan makes a compelling argument, however, that even the high and stable rate of private sector investment during this period could be attributed to business confidence in the stability of final demand made possible by the "Keynesian" role of governments. For all the failures to construct a strong and sustainable international monetary system, this was an extraordinarily successful period of economic growth and stability. It was a far different world from the frequent booms and panics of the classical Gold Standard era or the fleeting prosperity and then rapid disintegration of the economies in the interwar years.

ENDNOTES

Introduction

1. Robert Brenner, *The Economics of Global Turbulence: The Advanced Capitalist Economies from Long Boom to Long Downturn, 1945–2005*, Verso, London, 2006.

2. The usual distinction between goods as tradable items and services as nontradable items always had an element of spuriousness about it. To those who might take the sectoral character of the SuperCycle theory too literally, however, it does bear some explaining that just as the manufacturing boom in the East Asian economies in the early and mid-1990s fostered excesses in local services that sprang up around those manufacturing industries, so in the same way the housing industry involved a large amount of construction associated with it and developed to support the need for households to build up housing assets on their balance sheet.

3. The otherwise anodyne term "Market State" has been used frequently by a number of people, but Philip Bobbit's use of it in his book *The Sword of Achilles* (Knopf, New York, 2002) to suggest that an axial change in governance was taking place from the Welfare Nation-State prompted me to take the change one step further: why not a Mutual State?

Chapter 1

1. Makoto Itoh, *The World Economic Crisis and Japanese Capitalism,* Palgrave Macmillan, New York, 1990.

2. The efficient markets hypothesis (EMH) has become everyone's favorite whipping boy during this economic crisis. George Soros's *The Crash of 2008 and What It Means: The New Paradigm for Financial Markets,* Public Affairs, New York, 2009, and *Reflections on the Crash of 2008 and What It Means: An E-Book Update,* Kindle edition, Public Affairs, New York, 2009, have made a veritable banquet of Soros's repeated attacks on this rather thin gruel of a theory in financial economics. It will soon become apparent to the reader that I am after bigger game. Modern macroeconomics, which I have idiosyncratically named the New Equilibrium Economics, establishes relationships between asset prices and aggregate consumption fluctuations, and the efficient adjustment of individual preferences over risk and time in markets faced with exogenous shocks. It is this "structural" theory that I have attempted to call into question.

3. Axel Leijonhufvud, *Monetary and Financial Stability,* Policy Insight No. 14, Center for Economic Policy Research, London, October 2007.

4. N. Gregory Mankiw, "The Macroeconomist as Scientist and Engineer," *Journal of Economic Perspectives,* American Economic Association, vol. 20, no. 4, Fall 2006, pp. 29–46.

5. Michael Woodford, "Convergence in Macroeconomics: Elements of a New Synthesis," January 4, paper presented at the Annual Meeting of the American Economics Association, January 4, 2008.

6. Frederic S. Mishkin, "The Federal Reserve's Enhanced Communication Strategy and the Science of Monetary Policy,"

speech given to the Massachusetts Institute of Technology's Undergraduate Economics Association, Cambridge, November 29, 2007.

7. Milton Friedman, *Essays in Positive Economics,* University of Chicago Press, Chicago, 1953.

8. V. V. Chari, Patrick J. Kehoe, and Ellen R. McGrattan, "New Keynesian Models: Not Yet Useful for Policy Analysis," Annual Meeting of the American Economic Association, September 2008, *American Economic Journal,* vol. 1, no. 1, January 2009, pp. 242–266.

9. "The Crisis in Physics, 1904," *Scientific American,* February 1994, pp. 99–106.

10. Alan Greenspan, Testimony before U.S. House of Representatives Finance Committee, October 23, 2008.

11. Frederic S. Mishkin, "Globalization: A Force for Good?" Weissman Center Distinguished Lecture Series, Baruch College, New York, October 12, 2006.

12. Frederic S. Mishkin, "Housing and the Monetary Transmission Mechanism," *Finance and Economics Discussion Series Working Paper,* presented at the Federal Reserve Bank of Kansas City's Economic Symposium, Jackson Hole, Wyo., September 1, 2007.

Chapter 2

1. Ben S. Bernanke, "The Global Saving Glut and the U.S. Current Account Deficit," Sandbridge Lecture, Virginia Association of Economics, Richmond, March 10, 2005.

2. Michael Dooley, Peter Garber, and David Folkerts-Landau, "A Map to the Revised Bretton Woods End-Game," *Deutsche Bank Securities Research,* June 2004.

3. "When a Flow Becomes a Flood," Briefing, *Economist*, January 24, 2009.

4. Alla Gil, "Integrating Event Risk in Portfolio Construction," in *Credit Derivative Strategies,* edited by Rohan Douglas, Bloomberg Press, New York, 2007, chap. 7, pp. 123–140.

Chapter 3

1. Robert E. Hall, "Separating the Business Cycle from Other Fluctuations," Federal Reserve Bank of Kansas City, Jackson Hole, Wyo., Symposium, August 2005.

2. Individual economies within this framework could be thought of as collections (or "portfolios") of sectors. Large developed economies tend to be more diversified than smaller developing economies. Hence, the United States, although services dominated, also probably has more sectors from the global pipeline represented in its national economy than any other. Yet even with that diversity, the dominance of services—and of financial services in particular—delivered a crippling blow to the U.S. economy when the SuperCycle made its way to the end of the pipeline.

   An economy like Ecuador's or Angola's or even Russia's is dominated by a small number of usually commodity-related sectors. Of course, there also tends to be ancillary growth that occurs alongside these sectors. These (usually) service industries that spring up to support the dominant one will suffer the same fate as their symbiotic partner in the up and down phases of the SuperCycle.

   In general, though some of this is the result of endowments, globalization of trade and finance have worked to reduce these dispersions and increase concentrations of sectors within national economies, as one would expect from the workings of comparative advantage.

Countries that have a similar portfolio of sectors in their national economies will behave in similar ways at the same stage in the SuperCycle. So South Africa, Brazil, and Australia, due to the importance of their industrial commodity industries, will exhibit greater comovement at all times in their economies than, say, Brazil and Germany, or South Korea and South Africa. In the same way, the U.S. and U.K. economies will exhibit similar features in the timing, length, and amplitude of their fluctuations.

3. Ben S. Bernanke, "Making Sure 'It' Doesn't Happen Here," speech given to the National Economists Club, Washington, D.C., November 21, 2002.

4. Federal Open Markets Committee, Minutes, March 2003.

5. Federal Open Markets Committee, Minutes, June 2003.

Chapter 4

1. A. G. Kenwood and A. L. Lougheed, *The Growth of the International Economy*, George Allen & Unwin, London, 1983.

2. W. Arthur Lewis, *Growth and Fluctuations, 1870–1913*, Routledge, London, 1978.

3. Bank Credit Analyst (BCA), *Bullish Lessons for Commodities from the Gold Standard, Commodity, and Energy Strategy*, Montreal, 2009.

4. Charles P. Kindleberger, *The Terms of Trade: A European Case Study*, Massachusetts Institute of Technology, Cambridge, 1956.

5. Alexander Kirkland Cairncross, *Home and Foreign Investment, 1870–1913*, Cambridge University Press, Cambridge, U.K., and New York, 1953, and Arthur I. Bloomfield, *Patterns of Fluctuation in International Investment Before*

1914, Department of Economics, Princeton University, Princeton, N.J., 1968.

6. John Kenneth Galbraith, *Money: Whence It Came, Where It Went*, Houghton Mifflin, Boston, 1975.

7. Marcello De Cecco, *Money and Empire: The International Gold Standard, 1890–1914*, Blackwell, Oxford, England, 1975.

Chapter 5

1. John Kenneth Galbraith, *Money: Whence It Came, Where It Went*, Houghton Mifflin, Boston, 1975.

2. Enzo Grilli and Maw Cheng Yang, "Primary Commodity Prices, Manufactured Goods Prices, and the Terms of Trade of Developing Countries," *World Bank Economic Review*, vol. 2, no. 1. 1988.

3. Stephan Pfaffenzeller, Paul Newbold, and Anthony Rayner, "A Short Note on Updating the Grilli and Yang Commodity Price Index," *World Bank Economic Review*, vol. 21, no. 1, 2007.

4. W. W. Rostow, *The World Economy: Theory, History, and Prospects*, Macmillan, London, 1978.

5. Arthur I. Bloomfield, *Patterns of Fluctuation in International Investment Before 1914*, Department of Economics, Princeton University, Princeton, N.J., 1968.

Chapter 6

1. Michael Mussa, "Monetary Policy," in *American Economic Policy in the 1980s*, University of Chicago Press, Chicago, 1994.

2. Inter-American Development Bank (IDB), *Economic and Social Progress in Latin America*, Washington, D.C., 1990.

3. Graham Turner, *The Credit Crunch*, Pluto Press, London, 2008.

4. Robert Brenner, *The Economics of Global Turbulence: The Advanced Capitalist Economies from Long Boom to Long Downturn, 1945–2005*, Verso, London, 2006.

5. Ibid.

Chapter 7

1. Robert Brenner, *The Economics of Global Turbulence: The Advanced Capitalist Economies from Long Boom to Long Downturn, 1945–2005*, Verso, London, 2006.

2. Ibid.

3. Walter Russell Mead, *Power, Terror, Peace, and War: America's Grand Strategy in a World at Risk*, Vintage Books/Random House, New York, 2005.

Chapter 8

1. Stephan Pfaffenzeller, Paul Newbold, and Anthony Rayner, "A Short Note on Updating the Grilli and Yang Commodity Price Index," *World Bank Economic Review* vol. 21, no. 1, 2007.

2. Ben S. Bernanke, Mark Gertler, and Simon Gilchrist, *The Financial Accelerator in a Quantitative Business Cycle Framework*, National Bureau of Economic Research (NBER) Working Paper No. 6455, March 1998.

Chapter 9

1. Barclays Capital, *The Barclays Capital Global Equity Gilt Study 2008*, London, February 13, 2008.

2. Edgar Lawrence Smith, *Common Stocks as Long Term Investments*, Kessinger Publishing, Whitefish, Mont., 2003 (first published in 1924 by the Ferris Printing Company, New York).

INDEX

European Central Bank (ECB), 11,
149–151, 156, 157
European Exchange Rate Mechanism
(ERM), 149–150
Excess foreign reserves, as safeguard
against flight to safety, 49–50
Exchange Rate Mechanism, 141–142
Exchange value of currencies, 58–59
Exogenous shocks:
financial markets in propagating,
37–40
flight to safety/settling of accounts and,
34–36
Exuberance, signs of, 75, 80, 113–114,
146–148, 207–209

Fallacy of comparison, xv–xvi
Financial capital, as flows, 58–59
Financial innovation:
collateralized debt, 51–57, 157,
175–176, 205–212
and crash of 2008, 51–57
dividend swaps, 202–203
monetization of debt, xiv–xv, xix–xx,
115, 157–159, 181–182
Financial sector:
in the 1990s, 153–154
efficient markets theory and, 37–38
in propagation of exogenous shocks,
37–40
roles in macroeconomics, 6–9, 18,
21–25, 28, 37–40
Financialization process, xix–xx,
157–159
First Law of SuperCycle Motion:
Corollary, 109
described, 80, 83–84, 86–88,
126–127, 221
Fisher, Irving, x, 174–176
Fisher, Stanley, 140–141
Flexible exchange rates:
paradox of flexibility, xvi–xvii, 69
SuperCycle impact and, 69, 84–85
Flight to safety/settling of accounts:
excess foreign reserves as safeguard,
49–50
exogenous shocks and, 34–36
Forbearance of debt, xiv, 179, 210
Ford, Henry, xix, 154
Ford Motor Company, xix
Fordism, xix, 154–155

Foreign direct investment (FDI),
in benign view of global imbalances,
46–48
France:
deflation of 1873–1900, 91
end of Bretton Woods system and, 114
Triparty Agreement (1936), 122
Free Silver movement, 97
Friedman, Milton, 12–14, 29, 76, 156

Galbraith, John Kenneth, 97, 105
General equilibrium, 20
Germany:
central bank, 9, 129
deflation of 1873–1900, 91
as Gold Standard economy, xi, 214–215
Great Depression and, 85–86
growth of services in 1990s, 153
World War I debt, 111–112
Gertler, Mark, 174, 176
Gilchrist, Simon, 174, 176
Glass-Steagall Act, 38, 39
Global imbalances:
"America the innocent victim" view of,
44–46
benign view of, 46–48
in crash of 2008–2009, 44–50
Deutsche Bank analysis of, 46–48
Gold Exchange Standard, xii, 112–115,
132, 221–222
Gold investments, 204
Gold Standard, 213–220
commodity price deflation of 1890s and,
95, 105–109, 136
deflation after adoption, 91, 93, 105
floating exchange rates and, 84–85
of Great Britain, 90, 92–94,
98–99, 104, 105–106, 108–110,
217–220, 221
international spread of, 214–220
post–World War I "dirty" Gold Standard, 220–221
price levels after adoption of, 90–94
United States' commitment to, xi, 104,
105, 215, 220–221
U.S. dollar and, 87–88
World War I and end of, 104, 109–113
Gold Standard Act (1925), 221
Gold-Sterling Standard, 86–87
Gold-U.S. dollar standard (*see* Bretton
Woods system)

Arun Motianey was managing director and head of macro research and strategy at Citigroup Global Wealth Management until March 2009. He was a voting member of the division's Investment Strategy Committee from 2005 to 2007 and its Global Investment Committee from 2007 to 2008. He was also a member of its Asset-Liability Committee and advised it on rates strategy for its $2 billion unhedged portfolio. Motianey's 20-year career at Citi spanned a wide range of responsibilities in the firm's corporate and institutional bank as well as its wealth and investment management businesses, including head of investment research (2001–2005) and chief emerging markets strategist (1996–2001). Early in his tenure at Citi, he was an analyst in the Office of Chairman and a liaison with the International Monetary Fund on issues relating to the restructuring of LDC debt. Motianey studied mathematics and economics at Cambridge University, and his Ph.D. dissertation was supervised by the late John Frank Adams. He lives in Short Hills, NJ.